A
YEAR
TO
REMEMBER

Pictures and thoughts by James McSweeney

Thomas Crosbie Holdings Limited

Evening Echo

Published 2010
By Echo Publications (Cork) Limited
City Quarter, Lapps Quay, Cork.
A Thomas Crosbie Holdings company

ISBN: 978-0-9562443-4-5

Design and layout by Damien Callender
Printed by WG Baird

DEDICATION

I dedicate this book to Coláiste Choilm and Gaelcholáiste Choilm, Ballincollig. It is truly a privilege to be a part of the journey of this amazing school where love, energy and life bubble and overflow in abundance.

BUÍOCHAS

This book 'A Year To Remember' would not have become a reality without Diarmuid O'Donovan, Assistant CEO of Evening Echo. He gently steered this book from the camera to the page.

Particular thanks to Damien Callender who designed and laid out this book. His expertise is evident on every page and he has made the book so easy to read.

Thanks to the Evening Echo team of Tom Garry, Maurice Gubbins, Dan Linehan, Bill Linnane, Lisa O'Connor, Orla Keane, Deirdre O'Reilly and Brian Lougheed for their input and support in putting this book together.

A particular mention for my parents, Con & Nora, my sisters Teresa and Kathryn, my brothers Denis and Gerard, my nephews Daniel and Peter and my niece Aoife for their love and support.

Thanks to Bishop John Buckley and W & G Baird Printing for their help.

Thanks to Pat Kinsella (Principal of Coláiste Choilm), Cáit Breathnach, Michelle Sliney, Daithí Gallchóir and the whole school community in Coláiste Choilm and Gaelcholáiste Choilm. You are simply the best and it's great to be a part of your journey. If I have forgotten anyone my apologies but just to say thanks.

FOREWORD

'Dig within. Within is the wellspring of good and it is always ready to bubble up, if you just dig.'
~Marcus Aurelius

It is a great privilege to get the chance to put together this book *'A Year To Remember'.* It is three years ago since my first book *'A Year In Reflection'* was printed. A lot has happened in that time. Our own stories have moved on including my own. As our story moves on, it brings with it a whole new collection of significant and special moments. This book is the latest collection.

In a world that tends to be dominated by sweeping negative news there is a craving for good news and something positive. This book embraces the good and positive. All the photographs are a flavour of many moments that I have found to be uplifting and special. In each of them you will find the finger print of God. Photography for me is much more about capturing a moment. For me it is daily prayer connecting me with God who is present in the heart beat of our daily lives.

It is such an honour to get the chance to share these moments with you. Each photo is accompanied by a short thought to allow you to reflect a little more. This book is not a novel that is read straight through. This book is best picked up daily or whenever you need a little inspiration. Thanks to the Evening Echo for the chance to share this book with you. They have nurtured, supported and encouraged me every step of the way. I will be forever grateful.

JANUARY

New Year Celebrations: in Limerick looking across the River Shannon and St.John's Castle

JANUARY 1ST

'The problem we have living in this hurly-burly world is that there seems to be no quiet place where we can listen to God speaking softly inside the depths of our soul. Day after day we are grasping at this or that so that we might be secure and always failing because everything we grasp is as transient as we are.' ~Donald Burt

It's well known about the hectic pace of life. We read about it, hear about it, talk about and yet the hectic pace remains the same. But it's not going to change just for you or me. We must make such a change happen for ourselves. First and foremost we have to make it a priority to create some quiet time for ourselves. Any quiet time is healthy, important, relaxing and also sacred. It is sacred because God can be an important part of any quiet time if we so choose. As we begin a new year today the invitation is to be open to God in our lives. If we are open then God will always choose the quietest moment to make the biggest impact.

 Notes

Slowly: A car crawls down the snow, covered upper slopes of Mushera mountain, near Millstreet, Co. Cork

JANUARY 2ND

'There is a regrettable tendency in our culture to weigh Christmas with so much significance that it inevitably totters over and fails us or we fail it.' ~Anne Thurston

Today marks an attempt to return to some normality after Christmas. Many workplaces re-open today while our schools will wait until next week. It is fair to say that Christmas was yet again built up with huge expectations. These were so big that very few could meet or match them. If you feel Christmas let you down or has left you disappointed, you are not on your own. Was there any moment that was special or important to you this Christmas? If you have such a moment, be thankful and grateful. Christmas comes and goes but its message takes on a new meaning as we begin a new year. God continues to gently journey with us in ways we least expect and in ways we don't always understand. Such a gentle presence is not seasonal, occasional or by chance. It will be a part of every day and every moment of the coming year.

 Notes

Icy Windfarm: A collection of wind turbines stand out in the bitter cold

JANUARY 3RD

'Dedication is being able to see something through without taking short cuts and being able to pick yourself up after what appears to be a disaster.' ~Ernest Dillon

We all know how fragile a new year's resolution can be. The resolution usually isn't at fault but it's impossible to keep up the enthusiasm that's needed to carry the resolution through over a period of time. One resolution worth looking at is to dedicate my time and effort to some task that is achievable, worthwhile and positive in my life. The world we live in today programmes us into taking short cuts and getting everything done instantly if possible. But all that's achievable and worthwhile needs time and sometimes lots of time. The best new year resolution we can give ourselves is quality time, to do something within our reach and do it well. Why not ask God to help you as well to achieve what you want. You won't be disappointed.

 Notes

Live Gig: John Spillane at his best in one of his shows at Coláiste Choilm, Ballincollig

JANUARY 4TH

'The effect of having other interests beyond those that are domestic works well. The more one does, sees, feels and the more one is able to do, the better. The end result is a more genuine appreciation of fundamental things like home, love and understanding companionship'. ~Amelia Earhart.

'January Blues' or the 'January Wall' are expressions sometimes used during these early days of January. Trying to get motivated and energetic during these days is a task that many find difficult. The task for us is to get out of such a rut and begin to make something happen for us. It is about widening the horizon in terms of things to do. It's about taking up some new interest, doing something we have put off for a while, getting out for a walk and enjoying the beauty of nature that God has given to us in abundance. We ask God to bring balance into our lives in all we do, as we begin our journey through a new year.

 Notes

Heavy Raindrop: A snowdrop delicately holds a drop of rain after a January shower

JANUARY 5TH

I am grateful.........

Every now and then, I stop and think of you God. Maybe it's because I feel guilty for not making enough contact but I want you to know that I really haven't forgotten you. There are times when life is going well and I really want to praise and thank you for those times. Even when things are not going well, I pray for a plan and I know you are always prepared to listen to me. You know my needs, my joys, my pain and my struggles. You understand exactly what is going on for me. All others struggle to fully understand but not you. So I thank you God for being my guiding light that will never burn out. Although I may not always show it, I am grateful, grateful for all you have given to me, my family, my friends, my blessings, everything. Sometimes I simply forget how lucky I am and how grateful I should be. I just get carried away with life and forget. But not today and all I want to say is thank you, for everything.

 Notes

We Made It: Some of the wise men on display in the crib at St.Mary's Cathedral, Killarney, Co.Kerry

JANUARY 6TH

'After Jesus had been born at Bethlehem during the reign of King Herod, some wise men came to Jerusalem from the east. They said; "We saw his star as it rose and have come to do him homage.'
~Mt 2:1-2

Today the feast of the Epiphany is celebrated with great joy, particularly in many Eastern countries. Such is the significance of this feast that in some countries Christmas gifts are given out on this day. Today is also traditionally known as 'Women's Little Christmas' or 'Nollaig na mBan'. The wise men were searching for something they knew they had to find. It was a journey with many questions and a journey that took time, patience and faith. It was a journey that may have seemed futile and pointless. Why bother? Why take a risk? The wise men knew better. Today's feast day is a reminder to keep searching and to keep going as best we can on our daily journey, even when we don't have all the answers. Like the wise men, the end result is what it's all about.

 Notes

Free Hugs!!: Roisin Bohan and Emma O'Sullivan from Coláiste Choilm, Ballincollig enjoying a lighter moment at the BT Young Scientist & Technology Exhibition at the RDS

JANUARY 7TH

'Beauty gets attention but personality captures the heart.' ~Author Unknown

Beauty is so temporal. Take the example of a hard frost which transforms a landscape with a covering of a multitude of tiny white icicles. The early rising sun turns these into sparking diamonds with beauty beyond compare. Soon after, the thaw sets in and the moment is gone. The same goes with each of us too. Beauty gets our undivided attention and yet real and lasting beauty is often to be found within each person. Throughout the Gospel stories Jesus never judged by looks or beauty. He always looked within and often saw vulnerability, brokenness and fear. But he also saw potential and the unique personality of every person. People can take many things from us but they can never take our uniqueness, self worth, potential and inner beauty. Anyone who tries is a bully. As we journey on after Christmas, we must nurture and look after what is precious within. But it can only begin as soon as We start to believe in this precious gift.

 Notes

Breaking Through: A ray of sunlight breaks through the clouds over the Gearagh, near Macroom, Co.Cork

JANUARY 8TH

'A good plan today is better than a perfect plan tomorrow' ~Old Proverb

A young woman decided to redecorate her bedroom, but she wasn't sure how many rolls of wallpaper she would need. She knew that her neighbour had recently done the same job and the two rooms were identical in size. "Jane" she asked, "how many rolls of wallpaper did you buy for your bedroom?" "Ten" answered Jane. So the woman bought ten rolls of paper and did the job. Afterwards she found that she had two rolls of paper left over. "Jane" she said, "I bought ten rolls of paper for the bedroom, but I had two rolls left?" "So did I," Jane replied! A different question earlier would have solved a lot. It goes to show that a bit of planning always makes life so much easier. We ask God's help to plan as best we can for today, knowing that there is no such thing as a perfect plan.

 Notes

Out For A Stroll: A mother wheels her child through the National Park, Killarney, Co.Kerry

JANUARY 9TH

'I sense that the moment has come to commit all of the Church's energies to a new evangelisation'.
~Pope John Paul II

The late Pope John Paul II had his finger on the pulse with so many different issues that were going on in the world around us. Some of these issues were straightforward, while some were complicated and difficult. Many of these issues remain the same today, except that we are now living in a world that seems uncertain about what steps to take in the future. This is the result of so many setbacks in recent years, particularly the economic ones. Pope John Paul II called for a new way, new means and new methods. This is inviting and refreshing. It also applies to faith matters. The day we stand still with our faith is a sad day. We will always be looking for new ways of expressing and understanding our faith. Nobody has it worked out fully, but once we're searching and looking we are on the right track.

 Notes

On Ye Go: Eager and enthusiastic dogs at the start of drag hunt

JANUARY 10TH

'In any tragedy there is always a wonderful outbreak of care and help. Maybe God is the spirit of love and goodness that inspires people at a time like this. Could God be the one who suffers rather than the one who controls?' ~Tony Flannery

As chaplain to a big secondary school I get asked many different questions. One common question is why God allows so many tragedies to happen? My explanation is God never deliberately causes a tragedy to happen. That would be a cruel and harsh God. Then I'm asked if God is not the cause then why doesn't God stop or prevent it happening? Again this is difficult to answer. We often speak about God's love for us, who only wants the best for us and who journeys with us every step of the way. In any tragedy, God feels our hurt, pain, anger, grief and even abandonment. God is just as helpless because God can't prevent or stop something. But nothing can stop God's spirit of love and goodness in the middle of any tragedy.

 Notes

Teamwork: Action from the Macroom Ploughing Championship, Co.Cork

JANUARY 11TH

'A high recommendation is frequent, daily retirement into the solitude of one's heart, where separate from all people, you can lay open your soul and speak face to face with your God.'
~Francis De Sales

There are 1,440 minutes in any given day. Between 400 to 500 are given over to sleep. That still leaves a sizeable 1000 minutes to use positively and creatively. Many of these will be used for essential jobs and tasks that need to get done. Some will be used for relaxation and leisure purposes. How many will use a few minutes from the initial bundle for quiet time, silence and prayer? The benefits of taking some few minutes for essential quiet time each day are many and substantial. It is quality time and a time to recharge our inner selves. It is quality time that can be used to pray and to speak to God quietly. Prayer may or may not be on your agenda but there are very few genuine arguments to counter the benefits of quiet time each day.

 Notes

'Stop' A stop sign submerged in flood waters outside Tesco in Mallow tells its own story

JANUARY 12TH

'To me, God lives within me, God lives in my heart. The image of the potter is what summarises my image of God. We are in daily formation. Every single day, God moulds and fashions me.'
~Nina Isabelle Chillion

Pottery has been around for thousands of years. Each potter has their own unique style and finished product. But they all start with the same lump of clay. It may not look much but it has huge potential. The potter patiently works with it, allowing it take shape. Even if it falls out of shape, the potter will patiently start again. It is no surprise that God has been compared to a potter. Like a potter God works with us gently. There is recognition of our uniqueness and the something special which we all have. Like clay that sometimes falls out of shape, we also make mistakes but that is never a reason for God to push us to one side. We are in daily formation, constantly trying to do our best, growing and maturing, while learning new things about ourselves and others. Are you open to this ongoing formation today?

 Notes

'Wave Power' The Atlantic Ocean exerts its power at Slea Head on the Dingle Peninsula, Co.Kerry

JANUARY 13TH

'There is only one path to Heaven. On Earth, we call it love.' ~Author Unknown

There was a man whose one consuming passion was to go to Heaven. He had no time for the distractions of this world. Mass, hymns, prayer and work were the most important things in his life. Heaven was his full and exclusive goal, aim and purpose. Finally he died and went to Heaven. An angel took him by his hand and showed him the beautiful sights, the majestic mountains, lovely flowers, children playing on the streets, beautiful sunsets and many more pleasant sights. Then he said, "Isn't Heaven wonderful." But the angel said, "This isn't Heaven, this is the world in which you lived but which unfortunately you didn't give the time to see." It is easy for any of us to get so immersed in what we are doing that we fail to see the joys and blessings of life all around us. We need more than ever to notice, cherish and enjoy these moments.

 Notes

Pretty Pink: A colourful Gerbera potted plant adds lovely window colour in the middle of January

JANUARY 14TH

'Two antennas met on a roof, fell in love and got married. The ceremony wasn't much but the reception was excellent!!'

It's always good to be able to smile every now and then. The image of an antenna is a good one when it comes to things spiritual. We can choose to have our antenna open, be receptive and welcoming to whatever signals are out there or we can choose to keep it closed and withdrawn. Clearly when we are open to the gentle presence of God in our lives we are in a good place. The reception, or our perception of life, is then always much clearer. We are in a better position to make sense of the complexities of life. Like an antenna, all we have to do is be open and be receptive to the gentle presence of God in our everyday lives. The signals from yesterday are no more, the signals for tomorrow are not yet here, but the signals to be picked up today are stronger than we think.

 Notes

January Sunset: The sun sets behind the trees with fabulous colour

JANUARY 15TH

'Despite real differences and difficulties between Churches, the ecumenical glass is half full and not half empty. The fact is that the words of the Gospel are unique, universal and for all times.'
~Brendan Leahy

Each year, usually around mid-January, we celebrate a week of prayer for Christian unity. Down through the years so many divisions tarnished unity. Many of these divisions reflected the pettiness of human nature. In Northern Ireland great strides have been made in recent years to extend the hand of friendship across the religious and political divide. Our world today is made up of many faiths. For too long the emphasis has always been on differences and dominance. What's the point of prayer for Christian unity? It is a reminder that the emphasis is now on common ground and the strength of working together. What unites us is far greater than what divides us. At the end of the day we believe in the same God and its recognising that people do it in different ways. No one way can ever say it's the only way.

 Notes

It's Our Turn: After the snowdrop a crocus is sure to follow in the month of January

JANUARY 16TH

'We must learn to live simply so that others may simply live' ~CAFOD

There are many deeper questions that are often pushed to one side. They are pushed to one side because the questions are challenging and perhaps the answers even more challenging. One key question is why so many people across the world live in poverty and many in absolute poverty, particularly children. There are millions of people around the world today who are migrating rapidly out of rural poverty into western consumerism. It is hugely attractive. But as it stands there are simply not enough natural resources on our planet to promise a comfortable standard of westernised living for everyone. Any teapot including the biggest we know can only pour so many cups of tea. The "I want everything" attitude has no future. Everyone will have to rethink our values system and standards of living. It's not going to be solved today or tomorrow. But it now seems we have no choice but to rethink everything together.

 Notes

What's This: Hens at Tooreenbawn, Millstreet are a bit confused as they come to terms with something they had never seen before!

JANUARY 17TH

'The future lies before you, like paths of pure white snow. Be careful how you tread it, for every step will show.' ~*Author Unknown*

A wise owl asked a mouse the weight of a snowflake. "Nothing more than nothing", was the answer. "In that case I must tell you a marvellous story," the owl said. "I sat on the branch of a fir tree, close to its trunk when it began to snow. So as I didn't have anything better to do, I counted the snowflakes settling on the twigs and needles of the branch I was next to. Their number was exactly 3,741,952. When the next snowflake dropped onto the branch, nothing more than nothing as you say, and the branch broke off!" The little mouse scurried off with nothing to say. It may only be a story but it highlights the power of one, the power of something tiny and insignificant, the power of a kind word, a hug, a moment of silence, a moment of prayer. There is no end to the list or to the strength and power of something that may seem tiny and insignificant.

 Notes

Lap Of Honour!: These seagulls circle round in Fitzgerald's Park, Cork

JANUARY 18TH

Did you know....

The adult human body has 206 bones. An infant may have from 300-350 bones at birth. Some of these will fuse together as the child grows and so with years the number of overall bones will drop to 206. Of these 206 bones more than half (103) are in the hands and feet. The longest bone in your body is the femur (thigh bone) and is a quarter of your height. The smallest is in the ear and called the stirrup. Humans and giraffes have the same number of bones in their necks. It has been said that all our bones could be narrowed down to three to get us through life. We need a wishbone to dream with, a backbone for the courage to get through the hard times and a funny bone to laugh at life along the way!

 Notes

Soaking Up The Light: This Geranium leaf soaks up some January sunshine

JANUARY 19TH

'We should not forget that our faith is not something static but that it is always growing and developing. Perhaps not like a physical body at a static pace, but nevertheless it does so profoundly and at significant moments in our lives.' ~John Looby

We might say that these profound and significant moments are rare and hardly worth the wait. We think of moments like Confirmation, a wedding, a Baptism and other similar unique occasions. We might not put the following into such special occasions, like pain, disappointments, grief, hurts, depression and even betrayal. But even during these moments God is with us and never abandons us. Other moments may not make news headlines but to us they are important. These moments are life-giving and precious. Here too God is present and rejoices with us in the moment. All these moments, from happy to sad, all add up to being profound and significant. They nurture our faith and are a reminder of how close God is to us at all times.

 Notes

Winning Smiles: Eimear O'Sullivan, Aoife Cremin, Samantha Coomey and Aoife Power from Coláiste Choilm, Ballincollig enjoying themselves at Croke Park, Dublin

JANUARY 20TH

'Love is a symbol of eternity. It wipes out all sense of time, destroying all memory of a beginning and all fear of an end.' ~Author Unknown

There is a story told of a shepherd who once had a lamb that strayed too close to a cliff edge and fell several feet on to a ledge below. With the help of some other farmers they lowered the shepherd by a rope to retrieve the little lamb. However, the nearer the shepherd approached, the more distressed the lamb became. There was a danger that the young lamb might fall off the ledge. So they came up with another plan. They tied the lamb's mother with a net of ropes and lowered her down instead. Reassured, the lamb calmed straight away. The shepherd was able to scramble down, lift the lamb to safety and then its mother. Like the mother sheep, God always reassures and calms us, whatever our plight, storm or predicament.

 Notes

Snowcapped Mountain: Caherbarnagh Mountain is covered in snow after early morning showers

JANUARY 21ST

'I would say many people limit God and then don't look God up. You know, I think God is very much alive in every kind of person and every kind of walk of life and every kind of faith and religion. Because God is the whole of creation there's no way I'm gonna get a picture of that. So if I get your piece and my piece and his piece and her piece, then I have a fuller understanding than if we each have just one piece.' ~from 'Finding God Again'

It's one of the biggest traps we fall into thinking we have it all worked out when it comes to God. We never can or never will! But we certainly can get a feel for the bigger picture and that is a good place to be. God's beauty and love continues to unfold and evolve with every passing day. It is a privilege to get a taste of that each day. Such is the hectic pace of life we can often miss these beautiful moments. But God is indeed alive in every person, from every walk of life, of every faith and religion. The variety is incredible, amazing and unlimited. The biggest mistake of any religion is to claim ownership or exclusive rights. The wisest religion is the one who thanks God for their pieces but is also willing to embrace the variety of experiences of God that are out there. If each piece, viewpoint or experience of God is a colour, then we truly have an amazing canvas of colours. On its own your colour would stand out but within all the other colours it is the brightest colour of all.

Notes

Unfolding: A magnolia flower unfolds

JANUARY 22ND

Hannah replied: "I am a woman in great trouble. I was pouring out my soul before the Lord. All this time I have been speaking from the depth of my grief and resentment."
~From the first book of Samuel 9:15-16

Hannah's story in the Old Testament is touching and moving. For years she was childless and it was a source of great anxiety for her. Her story resonates with childless couples who long for a baby but for different reasons cannot have one. Such stories are heartbreaking. Hannah is presented as a woman of faith and courage. Despite her heartbreak at being childless, she never loses hope and never loses trust in God. Her story has a message for us too. Sometimes we want to throw the towel in, even to the point of wondering whether we should bother with God any more. Hannah, despite all her troubles, stuck it out. No matter how bad things might be, it would be a tragedy to lose heart in our loving God.

 Notes

Icy Roads: A concrete truck overturns on ice near Mushera Mountain. The driver miraculously escaped uninjured.

JANUARY 23RD

'We buy junk and sell antiques!' ~Sign outside a country shop

Where would we be without a sense of humour. Antiques are a thriving business. What we might see as junk is a beautiful and priceless antique to someone else. Every one of us has junk we could throw out or even recycle! Getting rid of what's old and stale has always been an important part of any spiritual journey. Such junk could be described as hurts, grudges, anger, hatred, jealousy, cynicism, mistakes made, to mention only a few. All of this junk can never become an antique. They are corrosive over time and are simply no use to anyone. God is always gently encouraging us to get rid of such junk. In its place we welcome God's invitation to new beginnings and possibilities, no matter how small.

 Notes

Bleak Landscape: A low setting sun casts long shadows on a frozen roadside lake

JANUARY 24TH

A light hearted story…

A farmer was trying to get his donkey to move on but the donkey was having none of it and refused to move. The farmer was getting frustrated, roaring and shouting at the poor donkey. Then he picked up a stick to whip the donkey when a car skidded to a halt next to him and out steps a stunningly beautiful woman. She gave out to the farmer, "How dare you shout and roar at this poor animal and worse again that you should hit him with a stick. You need to be gentle and give it some words of encouragement." With that she went over to the donkey, stroked its ear, rubbed its nose, kissed its mane and talked ever so sweet to the donkey. Sure enough the donkey happily set off on its travels. The woman turned round to find your man stretched on the ground. "Oh my God" she shouted, "are you ok?" "Oh I'm fine" he said, "but I think I need some encouragement too!!"

 Notes

January Smiles: Model Niamh Rigby is all smiles during a charity fundraiser for Marymount Hospice

JANUARY 25TH

'Sometimes we can go on nursing and hugging our hurt, wallowing in the memory of the wrong that has been done.' ~Aideen Clifford

Today is the Feast of the Conversion of St. Paul. There have been many significant turnaround stories throughout history and Paul stands high in the list. He was a bully, a dictator and a persecutor. He was mean, hard, cruel and ruthless, particularly to the early Christians. But significantly he put his past behind, did a massive U-turn and became famous for his missionary work and the spreading of the Gospel. We may not do such a dramatic turnaround in our lives but we can certainly leave some of our past behind. When we constantly dwell on past wrongs we give way to bitterness. Nobody likes a bitter person. Their company is negative, with little room for anything positive or wholesome. Like Paul, the call is to leave the past behind and look on today as a new beginning. It is the only way forward.

 Notes

'Morning Call' A blackbird is in great form

JANUARY 26TH

'It is always necessary to react strongly to what dehumanises society. It is necessary to join forces together to defeat all forms of marginalisation.' ~Pope Benedict

We are all a hugely significant part of society. Our contribution is important, valued and respected. Our presence in society makes a significant difference. But sadly it doesn't always work out this way. Many people feel they are just a number, that their role is limited, even futile, and that no one really values them for who they are. What a shame and what a pity. Is this a new phenomenon? Not at all. Back in the time of Jesus, he constantly met people who were unhappy, disillusioned and marginalised. He did his best to include them but always started by getting each person to believe in their self worth, their uniqueness and the unique contribution each could make. Today, the need is even greater to nurture, to encourage, to listen and to simply be there for each other.

 Notes

Time Out: Cassie a Corgi pup goes for 40 winks after some fun with a ball of wool

JANUARY 27TH

'Life is a process of starting over again. Every day marks moments for new beginnings and hopes. The comfort of our faith is that it allows one to let go of disappointments and missed opportunities. It teaches us that no moment is wasted and that if we think we have failed in our promise, the seeds of opportunity for growth and fulfilment never fail'. ~Thomas Keating

We need to hear more and more that it's ok to let go of disappointments and missed opportunities. The high rate of suicide today, especially in young people, would link it with an inability to cope with some crisis in life. There is a huge pressure to perform, be successful, be cool and to be far more than we can be. There is an onus on all of us to nurture every possibility of a new beginning, especially with young people. Failure and disappointments are part and parcel of life. We can use them as stepping stones and as moments of growth. We ask God today to help us seize such moments of growth.

 Notes

Friendly Snake: This baby snake was quite happy to get its picture taken at the RDS

JANUARY 28TH

'There must be something strangely sacred in salt. It is in our tears and in the sea.' ~Kahlil Gibran

Salt is something we can't do without. It is involved in regulating the water content and balance of our body. Too little of it and we're in trouble and too much also puts us in trouble. It's all about finding the right balance. There are 35 references to salt in our scriptures. It's no surprise that Jesus used it in his teaching. To use something that was so familiar to people was a great starting point. He said we are the salt of the earth. In other words we are crucially important, valued and loved. The main purpose of salt is not just to add taste to food but to bring balance to our bodies. So it is with us. Finding the right balance in all we do is a life-long challenge. Many long for this balance. Putting our trust and faith in a loving God gives us a great foundation to find and build this balance.

 Notes

Bleak and Barren: This tree stands out on the bleak winter landscape up in the Galtee mountains, Co. Tipperary

JANUARY 29TH

'Anyone who does not know God, even if he/she entertains all kinds of hope, is ultimately without hope, without the great hope that sustains the whole of life.' ~*Pope Benedict XVI*

This piece of wisdom offers plenty food for thought. It's not something that was made up in the heat of the moment but was given great reflection and thought. We often search for hope in so many places and often perhaps in the wrong place. Many think that hope can be bought, but money also has its limits. Can money buy real and lasting friendships? Can it buy love? Can it buy the freedom that simplicity brings? Can it buy laughter, honesty, genuineness and the freedom to be the best that God has created us to be? God is indeed the one who can bring us all these and so much more besides. With God we can have so much and without we simply have so little.

 Notes

I Can Fly!: Timmy Lehane from Aubane goes for maximum speed and height as he sleds down a hill

JANUARY 30TH

'Once you choose hope, anything's possible.' ~Christopher Reeve

A boy was in the burn unit of a hospital for many weeks making little if any progress. His teacher was asked to visit him and tutor the boy with some schoolwork. As she tried to tutor him it was obvious the boy was in a lot of discomfort. The teacher felt ashamed of putting him through such a senseless exercise. The next day the nurse asked her: "What did you do to that boy? His entire attitude has changed. It's as though he has decided to live." A few weeks later the boy explained that he had given up hope until his teacher arrived. "They wouldn't send my teacher to work on nouns and verbs with a dying boy, would they?" We too journey into people's lives and into places and events that on the surface seem to have no meaning or purpose to us. Yet God gently works through us, creating many surprises and in ways we least expect.

 Notes

Pushing Through: The daffodil pushes through with confidence

JANUARY 31ST

'Paradox is everywhere: Sometimes the things you think will make you happy end up saddening you, and sometimes the very thing that breaks your heart is also the thing that opens it to warmth and gratitude.' ~Ronald Ronheiser

Life can never be described as predictable and boring. So much can happen in a week, a day, even in a few minutes. There are so many twists and turns in life. If we are happy with our lot and with what we're doing, then we should be grateful. It too can change. Taking for granted what we have set us up to lose it when we least expect. It is comforting to know that sadness too has a turning point. Sadness is not always something negative or to be avoided. We know that God is very much in touch with our sadness and joy. All of scripture reminds us that sadness does have a turning point. Sometimes we have to wait patiently to know when the tide has turned.

 Notes

FEBRUARY

St.Brigid's Day: Christina, Kathleen and Sandra McCarthy work with a bundle of rushes to make St.Brigid's crosses

FEBRUARY 1ST

The eternal is not elsewhere, it is not distant. There is nothing as near as the eternal. The beautiful Gaelic phrase captures this, 'fighte fuaighte', which means 'woven into and through each other.'
~John O'Donoghue

Today is the Feast of St.Brigid. It is always a turning point after winter. You couldn't say that spring is quite here yet, but there is a growing feeling that nature is slowly re-awakening and responding. Brigid was so in touch with the rhythms of life and nature. Using rushes she wove them all into a cross, to remind us that all the different strands of our lives are connected. They are not connected by chance but by the gentle presence of God in our lives. God's many blessings are not distant but are woven into and through the many different activities of our daily lives. We pray to St.Brigid and we ask her many blessings on us today.

 Notes

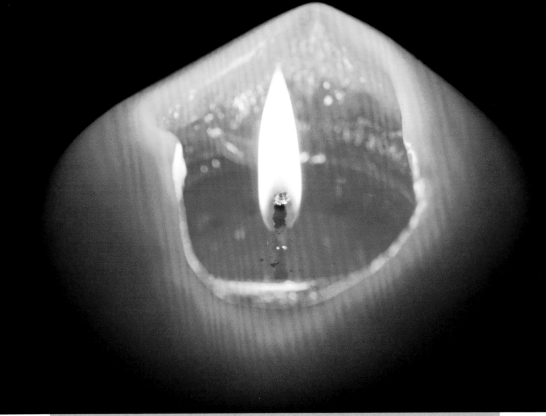

Candlemass Day: A candle radiates beautiful light to mark Candlemass Day

FEBRUARY 2ND

'If Candlemass Day be sunny and bright, winter again will show its might. If Candlemas Day be cloudy and grey, winter soon will pass away.' ~Traditional rhyme

Today is Candlemas Day. Like many Christian celebrations its roots lie deep in pagan times. The date lies halfway between the Winter Solstice and the Spring Equinox. It is a time of transition from winter into spring. On the Christian calendar it was renamed 'Candlemas' to mark the presentation of Jesus in the temple. It is a day that is rich in meaning and symbolism. We live in a world that is often darkened by evil and darker forces. We believe that the light of Christ is powerful and strong enough to wipe out all forms of darkness. This light knows no limits or boundaries. It's a light that is never forced but when we choose to be open to this light, great things begin to happen. Today we invite this light into our lives, into our darker corners and wherever such light is most needed at the moment.

 Notes

Evening Moon: A moon begins to assert its presence in fading light near Glendalough, Co.Wicklow

FEBRUARY 3RD

'Through the intercession of Saint Blaise, bishop and martyr, may God protect you from all ailments of the throat and from all forms of evil. Amen.' –Blessing given on the Feast of St.Blaise

Today is the Feast of St.Blaise, whose life was very simple and ordinary. Yet he is known worldwide for his care of those who were sick and particularly those with ailments of the throat. Blaise's protection of those with throat troubles apparently comes from a legend that a boy was brought to him who had a fishbone stuck in his throat. The boy was about to die when Blaise healed him. He was a physician who was very close to God. The sick came in crowds to consult him and some even brought animals as well. St.Blaise cured many people of their ailments and always sent them away with his blessing. He cured not just physical ailments of the throat but spiritual ones as well. We pray today to St.Blaise to heal us from all ailments of the throat, we ask for his protection and we ask his special blessings on each of us.

 Notes

After The Rain: Breaking cloud allows the sinking sun to cast beautiful colours over a range of hills known locally as the Three Sisters, on the Dingle Peninsula.

FEBRUARY 4TH

'Often the first sign of friendship is that we are delighted to discover the world in a similar way. We find ourselves laughing at the same jokes, enjoying the same novels, sharing other friends. We treasure the same things. Similarly we are God's friends not by thinking things about God but seeing things with God, through God's eyes as it were.' ~Timothy Radcliffe

Good and faithful friends are such treasures. We would simply be lost without them. Life would indeed be difficult, lonely and frustrating if we didn't have the company of friends. There is a world of a difference between a friend and an acquaintance. An acquaintance is someone we know through work or someone who lives in the same area. We may know many acquaintances but our real and true friends can often be counted in one hand. It would be nice to think of God as a friend rather than an acquaintance. As a friend God is in touch with our every need. Rather than someone aloof, distant and separate, God is someone who is close and near. A friend stays with us through thick and thin. As a friend God journeys with us through all that is good but is also with us through the mess and struggles of our lives as well. We thank God for our friends and we can include God on that list too.

 Notes

Bursting With Life: It's amazing how snow as a backdrop can transform a flower!

FEBRUARY 5TH

'We're building up or tearing down in everything we do. Are you on the construction crew or the wrecking crew?' ~Stephen Walsh

We all need building up in terms of encouragement, affirmation, support, kindness and positive feedback in the good things we do. These are the basic tools in building up any person's self esteem and confidence. When we choose to avoid some or all of these we are simply tearing down. Sadly there tends to be a fair bit of tearing down in the things we say. For some reason we find it easier to knock instead of building up. It is sometimes good to challenge each other and we all need it. But this is so different to knocking someone down through bitter criticism and sarcastic comments. It's hard to reverse mistakes made or regrets in how we hurt someone else. But we can certainly move forward in the spirit of building up. Can I do even one thing today in building up someone close and important to me?

 Notes

We Love Paris: Muirgen O'Mahony, Marie Neville, Róisín O'Grady, Aoife Quane and Sarah McCoy from Gaelcholáiste Choilm, Ballincollig are full of energy and fun in front of the famous Eiffel Tower

FEBRUARY 6TH

'There is such a thing as a prayer place and many people are very aware of that in their lives. It's a place where I can get away from it all. A life without reflection is not worth living.' ~Jack McArdle

We sometimes think that prayer must be confined just to a church. Anywhere else seems out of place. But we can simply pray anywhere that works for us. That can be in our kitchen, a bedroom, a favourite armchair, a favourite walk through a forest, along a seashore or even working in our garden. The choice is ours and there is great freedom in finding that place that works for each of us. It mightn't work for someone else but if it works for you then that prayer place is your sacred place. It's a place where we can simply get away from it all. It's a place where we can recharge, renew and reflect on the blessings in our own lives. It's a place where we can pray to God and share whatever is going on in our lives. Where is your favourite prayer place?

 Notes

Gentle Waterfall: A stream flows through some rocks high up in the Galtee Mountains, Co.Tipperary

FEBRUARY 7TH

'The old attitudes and the old answers have been shown not to suffice in this restless new world. At least one and possibly two generations have in large part been lost to the Irish Church.' ~Oliver Maloney

We can respond to change in various ways. We can hide and deny it or we can be open, welcome it and be energised. The Church has been slowest of all to adapt to change. The sweeping changes of Vatican II should have pushed the Church to the forefront, in adapting to the needs of a restless new world. Sadly, it stuck to old methods, attitudes and answers that were stale, outdated and often irrelevant. A lack of openness meant it was out of touch with a new generation of people. Many of these have been lost. But it's not all bad news. Reasons for hope have not been extinguished. There is now a slow shift towards a much more open and inclusive Church. This has to be welcomed. We pray that more people will continue to feel included and involved. We have come a long way-but there is such a long way to go yet.

 Notes

February Sunrise: The early morning sun allows the trees to look their best

FEBRUARY 8TH

The following is food for thought…

The most destructive habit is worry. The greatest joy is giving. The greatest loss is that of self respect. The most satisfying work is helping others. The most endangered species are dedicated leaders. Our greatest natural resources are our young people. The greatest boost we can get is encouragement. The greatest problem to overcome is fear. The most effective sleeping pill is peace of mind. The most crippling parasites to progress are excuses. The most powerful force in life is love. The greatest soother and comforter is prayer. The most dangerous pariah is a gossiper. The world's most incredible computer is our brain. The worst thing to be without is hope. The deadliest weapon is a sharp tongue. The two most powerful words are 'I can'. Our greatest asset is faith. The most worthless emotion is self pity. The most beautiful attire is a smile. The most appreciated word is 'Thanks'. The most contagious spirit is enthusiasm. To the world you may be one person, but to one person you may be the world.

 Notes

Hidden Beauty: The flowers of the gorse bush are nearly hidden under snow

FEBRUARY 9TH

'How will God ever make unity out of our extraordinary diversity, especially when each culture is so committed to its own pair of glasses?' ~Richard Rohr

A popular programme on RTÉ is 'No Frontiers' where we get a glimpse of many different parts of the world through the eyes of a camera and some good reporting. There is a great sense of how diverse our world is and how cultures vary enormously. Where does God come into this picture? Is our world just a random series of chaos and disorder or is there something more? Our belief is that there is indeed something more. God is always present in what is different and diverse. It is something to be embraced and celebrated. Yet at the same time we are also challenged to be aware of many inequalities in our world today. You or I will not solve these on our own. We pray for unity and equality in our world today especially in the midst of our extraordinary diversity.

 Notes

Take Off: Hundreds of Starlings take off with great speed and can often be seen doing many acrobatic loops

FEBRUARY 10TH

'Sickness is one of the real things of life and the manner in which we address sickness tells us something of what we think of life.' ~Archbishop Diarmuid Martin

We tend to push sickness to one side so that we can concentrate on the real things of life. Sickness has and will always be a part of life. It may be our story right now or perhaps some member of our family or a friend. Our response is always important. Jesus spent much of his time with sick people. He didn't preach to them or never told them to 'offer it up'. His miracles with sick people were not done to show off. His down-to-earth humanity, love and compassion is a reminder that he cared deeply about those who were sick. He reminded them of their dignity and that even in their darkest hour he would be with them. Nothing has changed. Every sickness is uniquely personal, a challenge and an opportunity. We pray for all our sick and for all who give of their time, love and energy in looking after them.

 Notes

I Can Fly!: Leigh Galvin is full of energy as she makes a flying leap into a bouncing castle

FEBRUARY 11TH

'Love is a medicine for the sickness of the world. It is a prescription often given and too rarely taken.'
– Author Unknown

Today is the Feast of Our Lady Of Lourdes and it is also World Day for Sick People. It is more than 150 years since Bernadette Soubirous saw the first apparitions at Lourdes in the foothills of the French Pyrenees. Five million pilgrims visit Lourdes each year. Anyone who has been there will know it's a significant and special place. Love bubbles everywhere in Lourdes. Its effects are felt by everyone. It is contagious, life-giving, refreshing and so alive. Anyone who has been to Lourdes will often say, "If only I could bottle what's here and bring it home'. It is at home, but it may not always be as evident as it is in Lourdes. Today is a day to make sure that God's greatest medicine called love gets shared. All of us are instruments of God's healing love. We pray today for all who are sick and we include doctors, nurses, carers and anyone who needs our prayers on this special day.

 Notes

Free Falling: A single drop of water is in freefall under a green lichen

FEBRUARY 12TH

'As I watch the news and keep in touch with places I have visited, I am more than ever grateful for a spirituality which never denies darkness and pain. The journey in life must be one of continuing growth and transformation.' --Esther de Waal

It would be great if everything was cosy and rosy every single day. Unfortunately, life is a mix of so many contrasts, happy and sad, elation and devastation, light and darkness, success and hurt, health and sickness, life and death. Every religion has its weaknesses but thankfully many strengths too. Christianity embraces everything that life throws at us and includes every contrast in life that's out there. We believe that God is with us in every good and happy moment but also with us in the darkness and pain as well. When we are in the darkest corners we need to know that we are not on our own and that there is a way forward. Our belief is that God is the one who helps us through what is painful and difficult. There are no easy options, no quick fixes and no magic wands. But one thing we are guaranteed is that God is firmly on our side.

 Notes

'Reflective Waters' Mallow racecourse is spectacularly beautiful under floodwaters as light begins to fade

FEBRUARY 13TH

'We need to plan and to trust. Act on what lies within our control. Leave what is beyond our control. Change what we can. Accept the rest.' ~Joe Armstrong

It is a natural instinct to be in control. We have heard about the longest journey beginning with a single step. That single step forward means we are in control, knowing where we are going and how to get there. But life often puts many things beyond our control. We can't control the weather or the timing of an unexpected event or crisis. Many fear that the 13th of any month especially if it falls on a Friday is a recipe for negative events outside our control. But such fear is built on other people's fear. Why choose to let others be the cause of your fears and worries? Today may be the 13th of February but I can choose to do something good and positive today. I can choose to do my best throughout this day. I can choose to make someone's life even a tiny bit better today. I can ask God to gently direct and get me through this day.

 Notes

I Love You: Two Red Arrow jets loop in formation to make a heart shape

FEBRUARY 14TH

'Love is everything it's cracked up to be. That's why people are so cynical about it. It really is worth fighting for, risking everything for. And the trouble is, if you don't risk everything, you risk even more.'
~Erica Jong

Today is St.Valentine's Day. The cynic will see it as a day of commercial exploitation and say the day is a waste of time, effort and money. But every day will have its critics, if given a chance. We often take for granted the precious gift of love. It's great to have at least one day in the year when we put it top of our list again. The challenge then is to keep it up there each day. Love, like the wind, is constantly changing direction and strength. It needs encouragement, time, effort, forgiveness, laughter and honesty. It takes a while to build up love, but only a second to loose it. You can't buy it or even sell it. It is up to us to treasure this precious gift from God. Today, St.Valentine's Day, could be a great day to start.

 Notes

Val: A limousin calf born on St.Valentine's Day was aptly named Val!

FEBRUARY 15TH

'We don't know how to look at God. We don't know where to look. We don't know what to look for. It is God in us that loves God. And all we can do is get ourselves out of the way.' ~Richard Rohr

It would be great if there was a simple formula in our search for God. We are often unsure where to start. Our searches are many, from our local church, attending Mass and saying prayers that vary from traditional to deeply personal. Some find that these simply are not for them and search elsewhere. These searches include finding God in the humdrum of daily life, music, reading, reflection, meditation, relaxation and so on. Whatever and wherever our search, it is good that we are searching. The one link in every search is that God is often closer to us than we can imagine. It is we ourselves who block this close bond. For years the emphasis was on God as distant and removed. It's time to feel the closeness of God.

 Notes

Power Of The Infinitely Small: A tiny parsley seed that was sown three weeks earlier has done its bit

FEBRUARY 16TH

If someone lives a cautious, fearful and risk-free life in order to ensure that they will get to Heaven, it seems to me to be a negation of Christianity.' ~Tony Flannery

The option of playing safe is an attractive one. Why bother if someone else can do it? Why take a risk if it's going to end in disappointment? Why try something new and different if what's old has worked before? Why be open to possibility when it demands time and effort? It's also easier to play safe in relation to spiritual matters. Playing it safe equates to not upsetting God. But playing it safe is actually an insult to God. God wants us to be free and open. We're encouraged to be positive and creative, to be open and honest and to love, even if a risk is involved. It's about living our lives to the full, seizing every opportunity to love and to do our best. Playing safe is certainly at the bottom of God's list of priorities.

 Notes

Gotcha!: A heron is delighted with its dinner-time catch at Dublin Zoo.

FEBRUARY 17TH

'I wish I were big enough to admit my shortcomings, brave enough to accept criticism, compassionate enough to understand human frailties, human enough to be thoughtful and open enough to be devoted to the love of God.' ~Gordon Taggart

These few lines of wisdom can best be described as beautiful and so appropriate. They merit careful reflection and can even be used as a personal prayer any time of the day. We sometimes need to be open and honest in acknowledging our frailties and limitations. Such honesty is not meant to be a put-down but more about giving us the opportunity to turn it all to our favour. The invitation is to take it to the next step and to be open to the love of God in our lives. This will always build solid foundations. Such solid foundations bring stability and a sense of purpose in a world that often seems to be spinning in a vacuum.

 Notes

Dawn Light: Early morning sun throws lovely rays of light through trees

FEBRUARY 18TH

'If you don't get everything you want, think of the things you don't get that you don't want.' ~Oscar Wilde

Much has been written about prayer. The value and merits of it have been well documented. But it doesn't always work for everyone and for some, prayer has left them disappointed. They asked for something and their prayer wasn't heard-or so it seems. But if you were to sum up all the great writings on prayer, all would say that every prayer is answered in some way. It may not be in the way we expected, it may not be straight away, but every prayer has some benefit and is never wasted. That's why prayer can be such a precious gift, not just to you but to so many others as well. Every time we pray for someone, we extend our love, concern and support to them. We may not fully understand why or how, but it's enough to know that God is doing far more than we realise.

 Notes

That's Mine: Elaine Scally from Coláiste Choilm, Ballincollig leads her school camoige team to victory

FEBRUARY 19TH

'Courage doesn't always roar. Sometimes courage is the little voice at the end of the day that says "I'll try again tomorrow".' ~Mary Ann Radmacher

The best of plans don't always work out. There is always some twist or some unexpected turn in our everyday lives that can throw us off track. If it continues over time it can get us down. Complaining, giving out and blaming others can often fall on deaf ears. But just at the moment when we're about to give up is the moment when we need courage. We need it to keep going. We need it to remind us that we most certainly can try again tomorrow. We need courage to keep us motivated and focussed. Many prayers have been put together asking for courage, especially prayers to the Holy Spirit. We pray for courage and strength to face everything we have planned for today.

 Notes

Breaking Wave: A surfer shows how it's done at Garretstown, Co.Cork

FEBRUARY 20TH

'Do not find fault with the person who limps or stumbles along the road unless you have worn the shoes they wear or struggled beneath their load. There may be tacks in their shoes that hurt, though hidden away from view. Or the burden they bear when placed on your back might cause you to stumble too.' ~ Old Irish saying ,

Everyone has their own unique story. For some their story is particularly sad and painful. We are experts at hiding or masking what's going on within. What is sad and painful may be hidden behind a brave face, or sometimes it is quite evident. Either way we need to allow for the unexpected and the unknown in someone's life. Something even as simple as a smile or a friendly word of support can ease a burden considerably. Instead of knocking or finding fault, I need to understand that there may be something of greater significance going on for that person. We pray for anyone who is stumbling along with some sad news in their life.

 Notes

Bitterly Cold: A snow shower transforms this bunch of daffodils

FEBRUARY 21ST

'Life is like a cup of tea. It depends on how you make it.' ~Author Unknown

When it comes to making the tea there are so many traditions. Some like it quick and instant, throwing the bag into the cup and hoping for a quick cup. The scalding of the tea pot is one that seems to guarantee a nicer cup. Some like it strong, some very weak and some middle of the road. Like tea, life depends on how we make it. Our attitude, our approach and our value system all make a difference. If we're going to sit back and hope that everything might come lucky, then we are going to be disappointed. If we don't put in the effort, we're also going to be let down. Each day is God's precious gift to us. Like making a cup of tea it's up to us to make the most of it.

 Notes

Forever Friends: This pair of swans take it nice and easy

FEBRUARY 22ND

Little Jenny was afraid of the dark so her Mum kept a night light burning in her room. One night the light burned out and left Jenny to face the darkness. The next morning at breakfast, Jenny told her Mum what happened, "It was scary at first. I almost called to you. But then I remembered what you told me, that I was a light myself."

We all have to face some darkness in our lives. It cannot be avoided. The first crucial step is to always remember that we are indeed light ourselves. Our faith reminds us that the darkest corners of our lives are never completely dark. There is always some glimmer of hope and some flicker of light. Today I thank God for that flicker of light and hope. It may not seem much but without it, we are indeed in darkness.

 Notes

At Our Own Pace: The McCarthy boys are in no rush on a February morning near Dublin Hill, Cork

FEBRUARY 23RD

'I will give you living water.' ~ John 4:10

The story of the woman at the well is a beautiful story that is full of meaning and depth. Jesus is compared to a spring of water, constantly bubbling, refreshing and revitalising. The Samaritan woman is drawn towards Jesus. She comes to see God's plan for her. She realises that it is Jesus who fulfills her deepest spiritual longings. She represents the confused person, young or old looking for meaning in life and wondering where to find it. She is the lonely person, young, middle-aged, old who is looking for love and who has looked for it in the wrong places. She reminds us how God's love reaches deeply into us and is a wellspring forever. The promise of Jesus to us is: "I will give you living water."

 Notes

Rolling Landscape: The lower slopes of the Galtee Mountains are beautiful in their own simplicity and natural colour.

FEBRUARY 24TH

'Much is sometimes made of the seeming lack of religious knowledge or adherence to Church teaching of the young. But you will often find them to be just as kind and thoughtful and, if we're truthful, perhaps also a little more honest than some of us from earlier generations.'
~Paul Clayton-Lea

It is sometimes easy to look at what is negative and forget the good and positive all around us. This is especially true of young people. Perhaps they don't always get 10/10 when it comes to Church attendance but they most certainly get many 10/10s when it comes to openness, honesty, generosity, kindness and a willingness to embrace what's new and challenging. Their energy and enthusiasm is better than any power station. Their sense of fun and friendship is touching. We've a lot to learn from them and maybe we need to give them more credit than we actually do. Today is a good day to pray for all our young people. We ask God to gently guide and direct them in all they do.

 Notes

A Special Moment: Mark and Niamh Murphy share a light-hearted moment with their flower girl Aoife

FEBRUARY 25TH

'Until you make peace with who you are, you'll never be content with what you have.' ~Doris Mortman

Much of the unhappiness in our world today has its roots in how we see ourselves. Too often we put ourselves down and fall into the tempting trap of comparing ourselves to others. God never makes comparisons or compares us to someone else. We can never live up to being someone else but we can live up to who God created us to be. We can begin this by believing in what we have to offer. It doesn't have to be earth-shattering but our little is all that God wants. Others may demand much, but never God. God always wants to extend peace to us. Can we make peace with ourselves first and in particular as we journey through these weeks of Lent? Can we leave the negative and cloudy parts of our past behind and move on. It is the only way forward.

 Notes

Woodball: A unique feature on one of the many walkways in 'Devil's Glen' forest, near Ashford, Co. Wicklow

FEBRUARY 26TH

Sometimes there is no need to reinvent the wheel.' ~Michael Ross

Vinyl records are making a comeback. When CDs came out, it seemed vinyl was destined to be lost for ever. But those who love their music will always say that music from a vinyl record is much richer than that of a CD. What was considered old and out of date is now gaining in popularity again. The same can be said of many things in life. We live in a world that has an instant appetite for gadgets and bits and pieces that are new and trendy. Yet not everything new can satisfy our deepest spiritual longings. Many things, like simplicity, peace, calm, love, healing and forgiveness, cannot be reinvented. These are precious gifts that are always within our reach. Sometimes it's easy to bypass what's near and precious. Today I thank God for all that has been given to me; much more than I realise.

 Notes

Time For Reflection: A gorilla is deep in thought at Dublin Zoo

FEBRUARY 27TH

'To solve the human equation we need to add love, subtract hate, multiply good and divide between truth and error.' ~Janet Coleman

Maths has been described as not making simple things complicated but making complicated things simple. Don't we all need to make things in life much more straightforward and simple. It is we who complicate life and make it so difficult at times for us. In our Gospels, Jesus spent most of his time telling people to keep their lives, their faith, their values and everything important simple and down to earth. This message is even more relevant in the fast and at times exhausting pace of life that we live at today. A good prayer today might be: 'Lord, help me to add some love in to some persons life today, help me to subtract hate and all negative stuff, help me to multiply all the good I can do today and help me to divide my time by using it in the best way I can. Amen'

 Notes

Home Sweet Home: A home made of sweets, chocolate and biscuits is the stuff of dreams for any child and was taken at Scoil Oilibhéir, Ballyvolane

FEBRUARY 28TH

We live in an over-stimulated, hyperactive age that makes the practice of stillness very difficult. Peaceful stillness is at the heart of prayer and union with God. It is also at the heart of wholesome sanity.' –Gillian McVeigh

We all long for some peace and quiet. We know it's important and good for us. But what we hope and wish for, doesn't always work out, especially when it comes to quietness and being still. Even if we look back on our day so far, we know we've been particularly busy and active. Sometimes, and maybe often, our busyness stifles opportunities to take things a little easier. One of the most famous lines from Psalm 23 reads: 'Near restful waters he leads me to revive my drooping spirit.'

Where are my restful waters? Have I some place to go where I know it's peaceful and quiet? Is there some space in my home that I can claim as my quiet time, even if it's only for a few minutes? Do I see prayer as an opportunity for peace and quiet? Only I can make it happen.

 Notes

Leap Of Joy: Aoife McSweeney is all smiles as she celebrates a unique day that only happens every four years.

FEBRUARY 29TH

'A Leap Year is added to our calendar to keep it working properly. The Earth travels around the sun in one year but in fact it takes a little longer, 365¼ days. The Leap Year every four years corrects this.'

The chances of being born in a Leap Year are 1 in 1,500. Any year that can be divided by four is a Leap Year. A woman can propose to her partner today. Of course for anyone whose birthday is today, it is indeed a special day. We too need to correct ourselves on occasions. We steer off course, we lose focus, we drift, particularly when it comes to spiritual matters. It is good to recheck and get going again. Thankfully with God we don't have to wait every four years! With God there is always a special welcome for us, we are loved and valued every day, including extra days like today.

 Notes

MARCH

Bursting Forth: New signs of life

MARCH 1ST

'It came as a shock to discover that in order to live well you might need to learn to read life. Life can speak to us through anyone. It can also speak without any words at all.' ~Rachel Remen

The ability to listen to life is a skill that takes a long time to acquire. It is a life-long task and one of the reasons why we are learning every day. No one can say they have it all worked out or that they are masters of whatever area they specialise in. The day we choose to stop learning is a dreadfully sad day because we physically close the door on all of life's possibilities. Everything in life goes in cycles. Life is fragile and delicate. Yet it bubbles with opportunities and energy. The person who has their finger on the pulse of life knows that it can go as fast or as slow as we want. When we choose to slow it down, when we deliberately pause for reflection we can begin to read the many patterns of life. Our journey through this month of March is an opportunity to find God within these many patterns.

 Notes

Parting Clouds: The clouds part after a heavy rain to allow the light through

MARCH 2ND

'Celtic spirituality is rooted in the simple belief that in all the unspectacular immediacy of daily living, both in the natural world and in daily work, God is close at hand.' ~*Esther de Waal*

Belief in God can never be taken for granted. It's a journey of many proportions. We may be really solid, we may be struggling, we may have given up or we may be willing to give it another go. Everyone who believes in God will be able to talk of at least something positive and beneficial about that journey. It's a place that is both comforting and challenging.

It's challenging because we sometimes have to stretch our boundaries to make sense of all that is happening in our lives. It is comforting to know that there is something more to life than just simply wandering aimlessly through it. The best progress on our own faith journey is to know that God is always close at hand and a source of renewal and life, no matter what is going on for each of us.

 Notes

Vibrant Colour: A bunch of heather flowers catch the eye

MARCH 3RD

'Books are the quietest and most constant of friends. They are the most accessible and wisest of counsellors and the most patient of teachers.' ~Charles W.Eliot

During the month of March, World Book Day is marked and in many countries the value of books and reading will be celebrated. With the advance of television, computers and technology we have pushed to one side the art of reading and the value it brings. Yet there is a growing awareness of the importance of books. The purpose of World Book Day is to highlight the many benefits a book can bring. We can journey through a book as fast or as slow as we want, but each visit brings many benefits. The Bible has the privilege of being the most-read book in the world. Today is a day to thank God for the gift of books and reading. We are encouraged today to simply pick up a book and start reading again. Even better again is to share the joys of reading by giving a book as a gift to someone else.

 Notes

I Love You: Two pigs show their affection

MARCH 4TH

'Some people are like garbage trucks. They run around full of rubbish, full of frustration, full of anger and full of disappointment. As their garbage piles up, they look for a place to dump it. And if you let them, they'll dump it on you. So when someone wants to dump on you, don't take it personally.'
~The Law of the Rubbish Truck

If someone has taken it out on you recently there may have been a reason. But no matter how valid the reason, it can never justify anyone taking it out on someone else. Difficult personal situations will always lead to a lot of frustration, anxiety and worry. It's important that each person off-loads this in a meaningful way rather than in a sudden outburst of anger. It is good to share our worries and problems with someone who is willing to listen. Part of the invitation is to also share with God whatever is going on in our lives. This includes worries, problems and all the unnecessary garbage we tend to carry around with us each day. It is good and important to offload some of these.

 Notes

Go Munster Go: Peter Stringer gets the upper hand against Glasgow Warriors at Thomond Park, Limerick

MARCH 5TH

Hello God

Hello God, I called today to talk a little while. I need a friend who'll listen to my anxiety and trial. You see, I can't quite make it through a day just on my own. I need your love to guide me, so I'll never feel alone. I want to ask you please to keep my family safe and sound. Come and fill their lives with confidence in all they do. Give me faith, dear God, to face each hour throughout the day and not to worry over things I can't change in any way. I thank you God for being home and listening to my call. Thanks for giving me such good advice when I stumble and fall. Your number, God, is the only one that answers every time. I never get a busy signal and never had to pay a cent. So thank you, God, for listening to my troubles and sorrow. Bye for now and I'll call again tomorrow!

 Notes

Daffodil Day: Michelle O'Keeffe gets ready for Daffodil Day which takes place during this month of March

MARCH 6TH

'My cancer scare changed my life. I'm grateful for every new, healthy day I have. It has helped me prioritise my life.' ~Olivia Newton-John

Daffodil Day always takes place during the month of March. Lots of money will be raised for the Irish Cancer Society. The daffodil is used because it is a flower of hope. It is found in every garden at this time of year and is full of life and colour. Cancer affects one in three people. There are over 200 different types of cancer; each has a specific name, treatment and chance of being cured. Cancer is sometimes known as 'The Dreaded C' but today is also a day of promise and hope. We so often hear of bad news but never enough of all the stories with happy endings. When you buy a daffodil, know that your money is going to a great cause, helping patients and families affected by cancer. We pray for all those who have cancer, we pray for doctors, nurses and carers and we pray especially today for God's healing. Information about cancer in Ireland can be accessed by calling Freefone 1800 200 700

 Notes

Camouflaged: A bluetit is nearly hidden in early morning sunshine

MARCH 7TH

'Example is so powerful. It is perhaps the most powerful word or homily.' ~Don Antony Sutch

We often wish for a better world. We complain when we see obvious injustices. We feel let down when evil seems to thrive and at times seems to be out of control. We wish, pray and hope that things will be ok and better for everyone. Jesus faced all of these issues too and tackled them head-on. He nurtured good news and spoke so confidently about the difference something small and positive can make. But he didn't just talk. He lived by example and his life reflected everything he spoke of. We may not be able to change the world, but through our good example we have the ability to profoundly change many things around us. We may say that's impossible. The response of Jesus is: 'Believe in yourself and all things are possible'.

 Notes

Sparkling: These flowers added plenty of sparkle and colour

MARCH 8TH

'Do not fear God who wishes you no harm, but love God a great deal who wishes you so much good.'
~St.Francis De Sales

There is great wisdom in the old saying that love is what we are born with and fear is what we have learned here. We have many fears, some of them realistic, but many of them unfounded and unnecessary. Some of these are fed by the worries and anxieties of others. Some are fed by bad experiences that can go back many years. Surprisingly there are people out there who also fear God. There is a sense that because we have failed and done wrong, then God is upset, angry and will hold it against us. The answer to that one is simple: Never. God wishes each of us so much good and love each day. Like warm rays of sunshine we can soak them up or hide in a dark corner. It is our loss when we hide in the dark. God can't ever force or pull us out, but the invitation is to always be open to God's love, goodness and blessings each day.

 Notes

Sunshades!: A cloud formation forms a sunshade over Caherciveen, Co.Kerry

MARCH 9TH

'God lit a candle of hope for each of us. It's not waiting in a window somewhere, or around a bend. God lit it right inside us so that we need not ever live one moment without it.' ~Vickie Girard

Hope is a word we sometimes throw around a lot. We often say that we live in hope or that we hope for the best. When the word hope is used to mean everything and anything, it can lose some of its impact. It never loses impact when used in a faith context. Hope is the voice that God uses to speak to our hearts. Hope is God's parachute in life and it is always God's smile. It is not a product, you can't buy it and it is always a part of a journey. In many ways, hope is prayer. Without it you have nothing and with it you have so many possibilities. During these difficult economic times we must have hope. We put our trust and hope in God to guide us through the unknown, to help us learn from mistakes and to use wisely the wisdom of those who have been there before.

 Notes

Keeping Watch: A robin looks out for earthworms as gardeners begin to get back to work after the winter break

MARCH 10TH

'We have probably overdone the stress on practice in our religion. In our gospels, Jesus was constantly telling the Pharisees and Scribes that they worried too much about regulations and practices. Instead he stressed: Look into your hearts.' ~*Paul Andrews*

The emphasis has always been on the need to go to church or go to Mass. It was a case of clocking up points every time you went and if you didn't go you fell down the list fast in terms of favour with God. Think of the guilt that built up around this way of thinking. It certainly was not the way Jesus would want it. Even today many grandparents and parents worry unnecessarily about their children not attending church. If you ask young people do they pray, (different to asking do they go to church) and the answer is always positive. Of course we need religion, Church Liturgies and a sense of community, but we also need to nurture the spiritual yearnings of many who are searching. The spirit of God is to be found in so many places. What a shame if we think there is only one road in that search.

 Notes

Eiffel Tower Reflections: Róisín NicCárthaigh from Gaelcholáiste Choilm, Ballincollig, looking at the famous Eiffel Tower in Paris as part of a school exchange programme.

MARCH 11TH

'We are sometimes vaccinated against faith. We don't get to the essence of it. We get distracted by our acquaintance with it.' ~Ronan Mullen

We vaccinate to prevent something and we only give a little to make sure something much bigger doesn't happen. In terms of what we believe in, we often seem to be happy with a vaccination of faith. We just take the bare minimum but in doing so we miss out on so much. Vaccinations prevent, but when it comes to matters of faith it's all about being open and being exposed to it. It is God's precious gift to us, it's free, never forced and always an open invitation. We have nothing to fear when it comes to the heart of our faith that God loves us uniquely. Nothing we may have done, are doing or will do can ever change this truth. Am I happy only with a little vaccination of faith this Lent, or am I willing to be exposed to some more?

 Notes

Confirmation Colour: These vibrant red colours stood out in front of the altar at Christ Our Light Church, Ballincollig

MARCH 12TH

'When you don't listen to the voice of the Spirit in the breeze, God will allow the roof of your house to be blown off to get your attention.' ~Garry O'Sullivan

It has often been said how God gently guides and directs us through life. We sometimes say, "Someone was praying for me", "God was on my side" or "Someone was watching over me". The Spirit of God is alive and active. It prompts us in certain directions, to try new paths, to be brave and courageous, to forgive and start anew. But we so often play the safe game and simply do what we think is right. Hindsight is great and it's easy to know after that we should have made better choices and better decisions. But let's not beat ourselves with blame and guilt. We need to forgive ourselves, move on and take a positive step forward. No matter what we do or don't do, God will never abandon us. God's gentle promptings will always continue. Am I willing to listen to the quiet voice of God?

 Notes

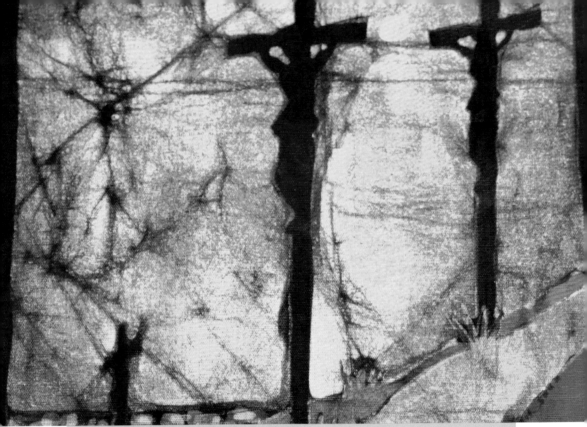
Lent: A colourful tapestry sets the tone as the focus is put on Lent at this time of year.

MARCH 13TH

'Pressure can burst a pipe or pressure can make a diamond' ~Robert Horryg

There are two ways of looking at everything in life and it especially applies to pressure. It's a word that comes up in conversation so much these days. Many people are under pressure and genuinely feel pushed and stretched. This often is the result of a hectic pace to life, the economic downturn, high expectations of others and sometimes just taking on too much. The image of a burst pipe or a diamond is a good one to explain pressure. It has to be said that there are few diamonds around and many burst pipes. The challenge is to let some of the pressure go before the pipe bursts. This can only come about when we honestly face up to the cause of pressures in our own lives. There are some we can't change because they are outside our control but there are ones well within our sights that need tackling. We pray today asking God to help us deal with the pressures in our own life and to help us off-load as many as we can.

 Notes

Identical Twins: Mum keeps a close eye on her pride and joy at 'An Riasc' B&B farmhouse, on the Dingle Peninsula

MARCH 14TH

'There comes a time in the life of every man and woman, whether a TV presenter, accountant, bank manager, cabinet maker or sportsman (in whose case the time comes a little sooner) when they have to wonder how long more they've got. Not in terms of the job, but in terms of life.' ~Gay Byrne

We all at times have to pause and reflect on where we are going in life. The currents of life are fast moving with little time to stop, pause and reflect. Unless we stop for reflection, we can drift along taking life, family and friends completely for granted. We can't do the same thing each day over a long period of time without making adjustments and sometimes changing directions in life. We can also do the same with our spiritual lives. We are encouraged to have a look at what's going well and what is not happening. There is always time to make adjustments. It's often the small adjustments that can have the biggest effect.

 Notes

Rays Of Hope: The evening sun beautifully silhouettes this old monastic church at Glendalough, Co. Wicklow

MARCH 15TH

'If you have a coin and I have a coin and we exchange coins, you still have a coin and I still have one coin. But if you have an idea and I have an idea and we exchange ideas, you now have two ideas and I now have two ideas.' ~Author Unknown

We cannot journey through life on our own. As we journey with people and those closest to us, we are constantly exchanging ideas, values and what is important to us. We may not agree with everything others may say but at least we have more information to make a better decision and a better choice. The same applies to faith matters. It's all about exchanging what's special and important to us. Anything that is loving and good will always search and find the same in someone else. When this has its roots in God, the end results are always productive and always to our benefit.

 Notes

'Holy Flowers' Clumps of daffodils in front of the Oratory at Gougane Barra in west Cork are a gentle reminder of spring approaching

MARCH 16TH

Sign on a fence out in the countryside: If you cross this field you had better do it in 9.8 seconds. The bull can do it in 10 seconds.
NO TRESPASSING.

Sometimes it's good to have a rule spelt out clearly! You would certainly have to think twice about entering that field. The same goes with many rules and regulations that cover different aspects of life. We grumble and complain about an unfair rule or request. But often there is a reason behind every rule and regulation that we often don't think about. There may not be a bull in every field but there are often dangers, pitfalls and obstacles that need to be avoided. We pray to God today asking for help and guidance. We pray also for courage to make the right decision even when it seems obvious and straightforward.

 Notes

St.Patrick's Day Smiles: Siobhán Swann, Darragh O'Haodha, Siodhmhaith Walsh, Rebecca Kearney, Lia Walsh, Conor Creedon and Andrea Raymond from Coláiste Choilm, Ballincollig enjoying a lighter moment!

MARCH 17TH

'There is a distressing tendency nowadays for people who should know better, to talk about Paddy's Day rather than St.Patrick's Day.' ~Cormac MacConnell

I'm not sure have you noticed it but it seems to be more common to hear about Paddy's Day. Poor St.Patrick! Is it a denial of what the man stood for? This included simplicity, bravery, conviction, courage and a man who always felt God was by his side no matter what happened in his life. Is reducing him to Paddy an attempt to say that his life didn't amount to much? He deserves more. Today is a day of celebration and thanksgiving. Life can be tough at the best of times and we need to relax and enjoy ourselves on this day. St.Patrick lived through difficult times too but at all times he simply put his trust in God. For some that may be a step too far but to give it an honest effort puts us in a very good place. Happy St.Patrick's Day!

 Notes

Make Sure You Take Me!: A beautiful Corgi makes sure it gets its photo taken with its owner Pat Casey at the St.Patrick's Day parade in Millstreet

MARCH 18TH

'When something bad happens to us, something that severely upsets our normal routines and knocks us off our normal course, the opportunity is there to question our assumptions and turn our lives around.' ~David Quinn

It happens to all of us at some stage when we are thrown off course by an unexpected event or crisis. We are human and vulnerable and we are all affected in different ways. The one common link is the phrase, "I took so much for granted." This phrase doesn't just apply to when we are thrown off course but it applies to us each and every day. We simply take so much for granted in any given day. This includes our family, friends, health and the many good things we still have despite the recession. No matter how bad things may seem, we can still get our priorities right and nurture those things that we simply take for granted.

 Notes

United In Hope: Two sycamore tree buds push their way forward

MARCH 19TH

'Good old days start with good new days, like today.' ~Denise Settle

How often we hear, "in the good old days." We hear of a simpler lifestyle, plain food and great neighbours. We hear about less money, more hardships but a greater satisfaction with life. We hear of more quality time and a better way of life. Some if not all of these have been slowly eroded with time, affluence and materialism. We certainly need more of the spirit of the good old days. The past can never become the present but the spirit of the good old days begins with a good new day like today. It begins with the realisation that it's we ourselves who are always in control of quality time, whether it is with ourselves, family or friends. I can turn the remainder of this day into quality time by choosing moments that bring me closer to God.

 Notes

Relaxing In The Sunshine: These new-born lambs are taking it nice and easy

MARCH 20TH

'And I shall put my spirit in you, and you will live, and I shall resettle you on your own soil; and you will know that I, the Lord, have said and done this - it is the Lord who speaks.' ~ Ezekiel: 37:14

These few lines of scripture speak to people whose spirits are low. These lines were written to remind the people that God would give them renewed life, hope and energy. All is not lost and in vain. The same applies to our lives too. Perhaps we too are feeling down and dissspirited. Maybe there is a part of our lives that is dead and going nowhere. God never gives up on us. God also wants to bring us life, hope and energy too. The invitation is to bring whatever is getting us down to God. We are invited to entrust it all into the hands of God. We ask God to give us renewed hope and life again.

 Notes

Spring Is Here: The broad leaf Poplar tree is one of the first to push forth its leaves heralding the arrival of spring

MARCH 21ST

'Pleasant words are like a honeycomb, sweetness to the soul and health to the bones.' ~Proverbs 16:24

Every person, young or old, famous or unknown, large or small, black or white, successful or less successful, male or female, who receives encouragement is changed by it. This change is always positive, good and wholesome. It is also at the heart of our scripture readings. The history of God's journey with people down through the years is a collection of uplifting stories. People were encouraged and instilled with hope, particularly when they needed it most. These stories continue today. A word of encouragement can be uplifting, it can strengthen and you simply never know when a few sincere words can have an impact on someone's life. Why not try it if you can over the coming days? Use any opportunity, to extend some pleasant and encouraging words to someone. They will be changed by it.

 Notes

Home With A Difference: Homes come in all shapes and sizes but this one gets full marks for being a little different, sitting on concrete pillars over the river Seine near Paris

MARCH 22ND

'They have lost the run of themselves.' ~Old Saying

Many of our old sayings are very interesting and always have some meaning. Behind the above saying is the idea that someone has forgotten their basic essentials. They have forgotten their values, their background and have forgotten their real selves. We might know of someone whom this applies to but on occasions we too forget the run of ourselves. We simply forget the really important and essential things in life. All of us are pilgrims on a journey. We sometimes forget that we are only passing through this world, that we are fragile and limited. We are not invincible. God wants us to do one thing each day and that is simply to learn to be ourselves. It's a great way of connecting with God and every time we do it, we most certainly have not forgotten the run of ourselves.

 Notes

A Dangerous Sport: A rally car speeds past another car that had just previously crashed, at Ring, near Clonakilty, west Cork

MARCH 23RD

'I praise loudly, I blame softly.' ~Catherine II of Russia

When a plant does not do well, we don't blame the plant. We look for reasons as to why it is not doing well. It may need fertilizer or more water. It may need more sunshine or perhaps more shade. But we never actually blame the plant. Why is it that when we have problems with our friends or our families we tend to blame the other person? We fail to look at the bigger picture. Blaming has no positive effects at all. It is often deflating, a waste of time and counter-productive. It is always much better for us to give our time and energy into words of praise and encouragement. Praise loudly is great advice but even better again is to blame softly.

 Notes

'So Fresh' A table of freshly baked bread looks so inviting at the Midleton farmers market

MARCH 24TH

'Now is the acceptable time' –2 Cor 6:2

How often we hear about keeping our feet in the here and now. There are so many options and possibilities out there today that it's easy to think a lot about the future and what we could be doing. It is much more difficult concentrating on what is just before us. A quick glance at any section of our scripture readings will point to God being present in the here and now. Our lives do not exist in yesterday or in tomorrow. Now is the only time God gives us for doing anything. Now may not always be the right moment, it may not always be the easiest but it's all we can work with. We ask God's help in making the most of everything that has been given to us, especially all that has been given to us today.

 Notes

Making Progress: A ladybird finds its way through the reeds

MARCH 25TH

'A teacher affects eternity. A teacher can never tell where their influence stops' ~Henry Brooks Adams

We sometimes categorise teachers with words such as: 'haven't they great holidays' or 'it's a handy job'. Such phrases do no justice to the great work our teachers do each day in our schools. We all take for granted their influence, the example they give and the depth of their enthusiasm and energy. No words can sum up the vocation of being a teacher. It is more than just a job and much more about doing something in life that touches not just this generation but future generations as well. We ask God's many blessings on all our teachers and God's many blessings on the great work they do in educating our young.

 Notes

Sparkling Raindrop: A raindrop sparkles in sunshine

MARCH 26TH

What do you want me to do for you? ~Mark 10:51

This question by Jesus to the blind man whose name was Bartimaeus might seem strange. Surely a blind man will want only one thing, to be able to see. Surely Jesus must know this and yet he still asks him. On closer reflection, Jesus encourages people to be confident in telling him what it is they want. He never jumps to conclusions about what that might be. Each person needs to be given space in which to express for themselves what they want. We might say are we not doing this anyway? It would seem not so. We live in such a busy and hectic world, that such a space where we can express our inner longings, doesn't always happen. It is so important to create such a space. No wonder it prompted Jesus to say, 'What do you want me to do for you?'

 Notes

Blackpool Blossoms: A magnolia tree in full colour at the Grotto in Blackpool, Cork

MARCH 27TH

'The first person who has to believe in you is you.' ~Author Unknown

It is always important to believe in ourselves and in what we have to offer and give. Surprisingly, many people are slow to believe in themselves. A child or adult whose gifts and talents are not nurtured will believe over time that they are simply no good. That is why words of encouragement are crucial whatever our age. We are often told that God loves us no matter what. But unless we first believe in ourselves, how can we believe that even God loves us? Whatever your circumstances, whatever your current situation, you have got to believe in what you can do. None of us can change the world at large, but my little bit can make the world of a difference. Our prayer is very short and simple for today: Lord, help me to believe in myself.

 Notes

Many Hands Make Light Work: Seagulls make the most of early ploughing near Cobh

MARCH 28TH

Jesus said to his disciples: 'Do not let your hearts be troubled. Trust in God still, and trust in me. I am going now to prepare a place for you, and after I have gone and prepared you a place, I shall return to take you with me; so that where I am you may be too.' ~John 14:1-6

We all know how racing pigeons can find their way home. When left off they don't fly straight in the direction they're supposed to go. Instead they will circle many times as they find their bearings and then they set off. It's called the homing instinct. We too have that within us. It takes the form of an inner restlessness and discontent. It is to be seen as a blessing. Just as the homing instinct of a racing pigeon doesn't protect them in their struggle with wind and rain, so it is with us. Our faith doesn't shield us from the hard knocks of life but it does give us our bearings. Our own homing instinct will lead us to our eternal home which is promised to us in the lines quoted from John's Gospel above. We may not fully understand what exactly this means, but it's very consoling to know in which direction we are going.

 Notes

Lapping Up The Sunshine: A huge oak tree stands proud and tall

MARCH 29TH

'God exists in eternity. The only point where eternity meets time is in the present. The present is the only time there is.' ~Author Unknown

One day a man asked God how long a thousand years was? The Eternal One answered with a wink, "Just a second." "Well then, Almighty," the man queried, "how much is a million euros to you?" The Creator of all shrugged it off with, "Just a cent". With an idea in mind, a gleam in his eyes and a flickering smile, he dared to ask just one more question: "Lord, all I want is just one cent. Can I have one?" To which the Most High All-knowing replied with a slight grin, "Maybe, in just a second."!! No wonder it's hard to win the Lotto!

 Notes

Back to Basics: Sausages are grilled in the simple traditional way over a campfire

MARCH 30TH

'If we want to be at peace, to feel good about ourselves and to celebrate being alive, then we need to focus in on the good in life. History has shown that human beings can be reduced or even destroyed by succumbing to evil, either by passively accepting it or by actively doing it.' ~Roy McLoughry

One of the greatest campaigners for peace was Gandhi. He often said on his travels that non-co-operation with evil is a sacred duty. He could see that evil destroys. He knew it had the ability to eat away at confidence, hope and our sense of worth. Today, evil has been glamorised through modern technology, television and the internet. It promises much but delivers on so little. Evil and wrong-doing are powerful forces that can shadow and even block out the effects of good news stories. It is up to each one of us to reject evil and to choose something good and positive in its place. Others may not be as enthusiastic but it is up to us to lead the way in nurturing all good news.

 Notes

'Morning Fog' A blanket of fog hangs low in the valley near Rylane, Co.Cork

MARCH 31ST

'If my mind can conceive it and my heart can believe it, I know I can achieve it.' ~Jesse Jackson

At the end of March the clocks always go forward one hour. But pushing the clocks forward means we can enjoy longer evenings and hopefully an improvement in the weather. We could also spiritually move forward as well. It could well be worth the effort, moving on from stuff that won't move with us. If we have done something wrong, if we have made a mistake, if there is someone who has been dragging us down or back, can we have the courage to simply move on ourselves? But doing so can sometimes be difficult. We ask God today for courage and guidance in moving on from stuff that may have been holding us back in recent times.

 Notes

APRIL

Inner Beauty: Beauty can be found anywhere like the inside of this tulip flower

APRIL 1ST

'Most of the things in life are simple and only the wise understand them' ~PaulCoelho

A big cosmetics company in Japan faced the embarrassment of selling a soap box that was bought empty by a consumer. When a few more of them were returned the authorities tried to sort out the problem. A massive amount of money was spent on x-ray machines in the factory line with high resolution monitors to keep an eye on any box that was empty. The system demanded extra workers and was still open to human error. When a small company faced the same problem, they went out to their local hardware shop, bought an electrical fan and pointed it at the passing boxes. Any one that was empty was blown to one side! Today may be April Fool's Day but we don't have to be a fool to know that the best and most important things in life are often found in small and simple packages.

 Notes

Nighttime Power: Night or day these wind turbines will work away creating lots of electricity for many homes

APRIL 2ND

'A book in the early 80s was named: 50 Simple Things Children Can Do to Save the Earth. An appropriate title today might be: 50 Things Children Can Do to Make Adults Realise There May be a Better Way.' ~Alan Dyer

We often hear today about the seriousness of global warming, pollution and the damage we are doing to the world. For many it is someone else's problem and so let them solve it. But there is also a big change in our mindset and for many people there is a growing inner belief that there may be a better way. Every country is different but Ireland depends on imports for 90% of our energy needs. Yet we could be well placed to become a world leader in renewables with our considerable natural resources in wind, waves and solar. The big swing towards recycling today by people of all ages reminds us that there may be a way forward. As a part of God's family it is vital we all play our part, not just for ourselves but for our children, our grandchildren and all the generations to come after us.

 Notes

April Blossoms: These apple tree blossoms are bursting with colour

APRIL 3RD

'Wishing is something we do quite early in life. Healthy wishing enables us to move beyond the past and the present. It spurs us to set goals for the future and encourages us to use our time and talents to work towards their achievement.' ~Melanie Svoboda

We often wish, hope and pray at the same time. Sometimes we get it all wrong. The loyal fans of two opposing teams at a match will be wishing and praying that their team will win. There will be inevitable disappointments! A healthy wish for something good and positive is always an important part of our spiritual journey. Clearly a wish must have boundaries but every wish bears the seed for improvement. Every wish points to our need for God. What is our wish today? If we wish for a glimpse of God's love for us, we will not be disappointed. If we wish for some courage, strength, hope, light, belief, forgiveness and healing, we will get some. A wish means a part of us wants to improve. Today is a great day to begin, with even a small improvement in our lives.

 Notes

Wedding Smiles: Áine Cummins from Ballinlough, Cork is all smiles at Fota Gardens and why wouldn't she with four enthusiastic lads looking after her!

APRIL 4TH

'Behind every face there is a unique world that no one else can see. This is the mystery of individuality. The shape of each soul is different. No one else feels your life the way you do. No one else sees or hears the world as you do. The creation of the individual is a divine masterpiece.' ~John O'Donohue

It is nearly an impossible task to get across our own uniqueness, our individuality and what we have to give. God has given us a unique fingerprint, a unique DNA identity and has given us something special to do in this world. If someone else could do it they would be here and not us. But so often we run away, we hide and we say we're not ready, we're no good and let somebody else do what needs to be done. But only we can do it. Our contribution is hugely important. The invitation each day is to begin to believe and especially in ourselves. God always believes in our potential, our progress, our contribution and our longing to do our best. No one can ever take that from us.

 Notes

My Resting Place: A raindrop sits delicately on top of this little fir branch

APRIL 5TH

'Think of farmers, how patiently they wait for the precious fruit of the ground, until it has had the spring and autumn rains. You too must be patient. Do not loose heart.' ~James 5:7

April unlike other months is not named to commemorate anybody or anything special. It gets its name from a Latin word, 'Aprilis' which means 'to open'. This is a very appropriate name because nature is indeed opening up to new life all around. We too are invited to open up to new life in our daily lives. It's easy to be closed and remain so because of hectic schedules. But to be open to new life, new beginnings, new challenges and new ideas is indeed to be open to God. To be open and to be in touch with the beauty of nature is also to be close to God. We are called to be patient and not to loose heart. April is a great starting point on that journey.

 Notes

Beyond The Briars: Great inner beauty lies beyond the briars with this colourful chaffinch

APRIL 6TH

'We just manage to hold on and often do not control our life. We allow it to carry us where it wants to take us.' ~John Looby

'Life is what we make it' is a saying that is often used and repeated. Every day is made up of so many possibilities, options, moments and decisions. The frequency and intensity of them make the pace of life hectic. It seems we are not in control and at times drifting helplessly along. But why is it that some people seem in control and seem to be totally connected to life, picking and choosing what and when they want it? Is it a life skill that some have naturally and for others one to learn? In our Gospels, Jesus showed his disciples and friends how to prioritise and choose life-giving moments. Instead of drifting aimlessly along he encouraged them to celebrate every bit of good news in their lives. He encouraged them to be creative, to have courage to say no when required and to always set time aside for personal reflection, prayer and time out. Small adjustments mean we will always be much more in control.

 Notes

Tall And Upright: These tulips look pretty and elegant

APRIL 7TH

Strength v Courage

It takes strength to be firm. It takes courage to be gentle.

It takes strength to stand guard. It takes courage to let down your guard.

It takes strength to conquer. It takes courage to surrender.

It takes strength to be certain. It takes courage to have doubt.

It takes strength to fit in. It takes courage to stand out.

It takes strength to hide your own pains. It takes courage to show them.

It takes strength to endure abuse. It takes courage to stop it.

It takes strength to stand alone. It takes courage to lean on another.

It takes strength to love. It takes courage to be loved.

It takes strength to survive. It takes courage to live.

 Notes

Just One More Go!: A surfer heads back to the water again at Tramore beach, in lovely evening sunlight

APRIL 8TH

'No one ever finds life worth living. One always has to make it worth living.' ~Richard Feeley

Life has often been compared to a gift and it is a very good image, except that at times we just look only at the wrapping paper. We need to go deeper and appreciate the special gift that it is. As we grow older we get a greater sense of the complexities of life and also a sense that all these complexities usually work themselves out in their own time. Quick fix solutions are very scarce. Life, we are told, will meet us half-way. But we often have to go more than half way. We have to make life work, we have to do our bit and we have to keep taking those steps forward. It is easy to be bitter, cynical, critical, hostile and angry with life, but there are no gains with such an outlook on life. Our spiritual beliefs help us to make sense of life and its complexities. Most importantly they help us stay on the road of openness, trying to make life work, doing our best and trying to help others along the same road.

 Notes

Team Workout: These cyclists continue the climb into the Wicklow mountains near Sally's Gap

APRIL 9TH

'Life is a succession of crises and moments when we have to rediscover who we are and what we really want.' ~Jean Vanier

For a cyclist it is always easier to cycle with other riders who will take turns in breaking through a headwind and make it easier to keep the momentum up. A lone breakaway cyclist will always have to work harder on a solo break and will have to do all the work breaking through any headwind. The same can be said of us too. Sometimes when we move out of the safety and protection of others or when we do a solo run we are open to feeling the elements more. It is at this time that we begin to understand more about ourselves, our limits and where we want to go. But it is always good to come back into the strength of team, family and community. God encourages us to maximise the support structures around us. Is there any person I know who needs my support at this time? Can I support them with some of my time, love and energy?

 Notes

'Flying Through' These entertainers show how it's done and enthral the crowds at the NEC Killarney

APRIL 10TH

'In seeking solutions, the world works from the outside in and Jesus works from the inside out. The world would take people out of the slums. Jesus takes the slums out of the people and then takes them out of the slums.' ~Harold Buetow

We live in a world with a big emphasis on the externals. How we look, what we wear, where we live, what we drive and even how we speak are on the list of what's important. Sadly there is not enough emphasis on the person within, on our potential within and on those many areas where we need a lift. Within each of us there are areas that need healing, areas that need letting go and areas that need space for new beginnings. Jesus right throughout our Gospel stories placed the emphasis on the person within. He always began by healing, forgiving and encouraging. He instilled confidence in each person and allowed them to believe in themselves. Then he worked on the problem that was dragging the person down. The problem was often well gone after he worked from the inside out. It's a mindset we could all adapt and one that makes a lot of sense.

 Notes

100% Concentration: Rebecca Kearney from Coláiste Choilm shows how it's done to win the Junior All-Ireland Football Final

APRIL 11TH

'Is prayer your steering wheel or your spare tyre?' ~Corrie Brown

We have heard on many occasions about the importance of prayer. We are told it's life-giving, spiritually nourishing, good for our spiritual well-being and an important connection with God. Another conclusion is that there are a variety of ways of praying and each one as important as the next. It's all about what works for each of us. Sometimes it's the short, honest and simple prayers that can mean much more than long lists of words. We know prayer is important and beneficial but it's only we who can answer that all important question: Is prayer our steering wheel or is it our spare tyre?

 Notes

Churning Up The Mud: John McElhinney churns up the mud as he turns the corners quicker than any F1 driver!

APRIL 12TH

If you take a glass of water and pour a drop of ink into it, the water will quickly become discoloured all the way through. If you take a stone or pebble and drop it into the same glass of water, it will fall to the bottom and remain in that position. It will not cloud or discolour the water.

The same goes with a worry, problem, concern or something negative in our own lives. We have two choices. Like the ink we can let it cloud and taint the whole of our lives or like the stone we can contain it, deal with it and not allow it take over our lives. A lot of news items tend to be sensationalised. All the soap programmes tend to thrive on sensationalism. If it's not sensational or dramatic it is classed as boring and dull. So over time we have got used to dealing with issues and problems like ink. We allow and let them take over our lives. This need never happen. Today we ask God to help us deal with whatever problem or worries we may have. Like the image of the stone/ink, we ask God to help us keep everything in perspective and not allow what's negative to take over our lives.

 Notes

Proud Of My Family: A cat called Patch stretches out to allow her three kittens

APRIL 13TH

'When we are losing, we run faster' ~Gerard May

No one likes to lose, not just in sport but in every aspect of life. When we are frightened or afraid we tend to panic and run faster. It is no coincidence that the pace of life is hectic today. Why is this so? Is there a sense that we are losing something? Have we lost the heartbeat of life? The faster we run in life, the less chance there is of connecting with what's essential and important in life. Mother Teresa put it so well when she said that few of us can do great things but all of us can do small things with great love. Can I make time for the small things in life? Can I do one small thing well today and be content with whatever this might be? Can I be reassured that it's more than enough in God's eyes? Doing these with love is indeed the heartbeat of life.

 Notes

Intimate Moment: Mary Nolan and her daughter Niamh share some special time together

APRIL 14TH

'I want to see the world through your eyes.' ~Pope John 23rd

Much has been written about Pope John 23rd and the sweeping changes of Vatican II. But one of the first things he did when he was elected Pope was to visit the large prison, Regina Caeli, on the outskirts of Rome. He quickly won the hearts of his prisoner audience by telling them that a couple of his own relatives had done time in prison and came to no lasting harm. Then he told them "I want my heart to be close to yours. I want to see the world through your eyes". Those words can still be found inscribed on a plaque in the prison chapel. Those words are worth reflecting for us as well. We can never assume anything about anyone. To fully understand someone we must see their world through their eyes. For every person this is different. It needs to be respected and can never be taken for granted.

 Notes

Kitchen Views: A pony called Toffee keeps an eye on proceedings from an old house

APRIL 15TH

'Guard well your spare moments. They are like uncut diamonds. Discard them and their value will never be known. Improve them and they will become the brightest gems.' ~Ralph Waldo Emerson

If we only say 'I never have a spare moment' then we really have pushed ourselves to the limits. Such is the hectic pace of life that spare moments are often squeezed out. This is a pity. We are the losers if this happens to us. Spare moments are ours to do what we want and where we want. We can discard them, we can waste them but they are ours to make the most of. Spare moments can be used for quiet reflection, for prayer, for a walk, for rest, for a word of thanks or encouragement. When used in this way they are indeed gems. A spare moment just to be still is also a gem. They are ours to hold and to use. How are you going to use yours today?

 Notes

Sweet Smiles: Helen Donaldson has every reason to smile with such a selection at Vernon, near Paris

APRIL 16TH

'Ring the bells that still can ring. There is cracks in everything, that's how the light gets in.'
~Leonard Cohen

The image of a crack is a powerful one. A crack is often seen in negative terms. It's something we see as a task, something that needs to be repaired. We sometimes speak of a crack in our lives, some area where we are struggling and an area we would like to improve. But every crack has the ability to let the light in. From God's point of view we take it a step further and say that this light has the ability to penetrate our deepest darkness. Darkness and evil can never win the battles of our daily lives. At times it may seem they have the upper hand but our faith and belief in God shatters this notion. Today we invite God's light into all the cracks in our lives.

Notes

Cascading Waters: A small stream creates a lovely peaceful setting

APRIL 17TH

'Last night, as I lay sleeping, I dreamt that I had a beehive here inside my heart. And the golden bees were making white combs and sweet honey from my old failures.' ~Antonio Machado

We dream five times during any night. Dreams are the one common language of our world. They unite humanity. They keep us balanced and help us function well and normal as a human being. But we so often undervalue our dreams. Throughout scripture there are many dreams where God passes on important information. All our dreams are our friends, are always on our side and never our enemy. Even nightmares are on our side and are simply trying to wake us up to something in our everyday lives. A dream will always deliver a gift to you. We need to get in touch with our dreams more, or even write them down. It's only you can say with certainty what meaning your dream may hold. Why not share your dreams with people you care about? Ask them about their dreams.

 Notes

Work Of Art: A birds nest is built with great care and precision

APRIL 18TH

Jesus said: "I am the gate. Anyone who enters through me will be safe. They will go freely in and out and be sure of finding pasture". ~John 10:8-10

Gates as we know come in all shapes and sizes. A gate can either let you in or keep you out. Today we see more and more of big electric gates in front of homes. These have been put in as an added measure of security, but sadly they can also keep people out as well. In our piece from scripture today Jesus gently reminds us that he is like a gate and the beautiful reassuring words that 'whoever enters through his gate will be safe'. We can make these words our own. No matter what our circumstances, what we may have done there will always be a welcome for us. We are also reminded of the freedom that is offered to us by entering this gate and of finding meaning and fulfilment. No one is going to be forced through the gate but for anyone who is willing to cross the threshold the rewards are many.

 Notes

Milking Time: A farmer and his dog bring the cows in for milking time

APRIL 19TH

'A young man went to a great master of wisdom and said to him, 'Master, so great is my trust in God that I didn't even hitch my camel out there. I left it to God's providence, for God to take care of it. And the wise master said, 'Go back outside and tie your camel to the post, you nincompoop! There's no point in inconveniencing God with something that you can do yourself.' ~Anthony de Mello

Think about all the inconveniences we cause others by asking them to do things that we could easily do ourselves. When we're spoon-fed often it's easy to see why we take things and people for granted. The same can be said of faith matters. Do I knock on God's door with silly stuff? Do I expect God to do everything for me? When we have high expectations then we are open to big disappointments. Maybe we need to trust more in what we can do and to know that we are doing it well.

 Notes

Hidden Treasures: A flower opens up to reveal great beauty within

APRIL 20TH

'What's the point of the Resurrection? Does Jesus risen from the dead make all the difference in the world or none whatsoever? ~Vincent Travers

There is a story told about a child hearing an approaching storm and muttering, "I'm afraid of storms". Her parents reassure her, "You don't have to worry. God will be there right with you." She goes upstairs to her bedroom and again the thunder rolls. She calls downstairs, "I'm still scared." And the answer came back, "You don't have to worry. God will be there right with you." At that moment the room lit up and this time she cried out: "I need a God with some skin on!" With that her parents rushed up, hugged her and became the God with some skin on. It's a lovely story that gets across no end how each of us puts skin on God. We put the human face on God and especially by our love, the way we live, acts of kindness, a smile and often a mixture of many small little gestures.

 Notes

A Different World: These fishermen have chosen a good location to relax on Lough Allua, Ballingeary, west Cork

APRIL 21ST

'Come now, put aside your business for a while, take refuge for a little from your tumultuous thoughts, cast off your cares and let your burdensome distractions wait. Take some leisure time with God and rest awhile with God.' ~*St. Anselm*

Today is the Feast of St.Anselm who lived over a thousand years ago and was a great thinker and writer of his time. But even back then he recognised a great need to take a step back from all we do and to take time to reflect. A quick response might be to say that such stuff is reserved for saints and all those who have a halo round their heads! But it's a basic need in every human person to pause, reflect, unwind and allow God to nourish our human spirit in some way. Some can do it through prayer but it's not the only way. Anyone who can take a few steps aside from the hectic pace of life in whatever way is doing themselves a great favour.

 Notes

Camera Cake: A birthday cake made by Mags Guilfoy in the shape of an eye-catching camera.

APRIL 22ND

'If in these critical times we are living through, if the questions that are absolutely fundamental to the existence of life are not being asked, then we all suffocate on peripheral and trivial obsessions, abandoning and abdicating from the very purpose for which we exist.' ~Mark Ballabon

It's true we take a lot for granted. Our hearts beat an extraordinary 100,000 times a day. There are 100,000 miles of blood vessels in our body. There are 100 million light-sensitive cells on the retina of our eyes. Our brains can make thousands of calculations in a second while only using the same amount of power as a 10watt bulb. We can distinguish over 4,000 smells and we can see stars that are million of miles away. In the middle of all these interesting statistics we have our own unique finger print and DNA. Our bodies are truly extraordinary and yet we often trivialise much of what we do because we simply take so much for granted. Everything around us just doesn't happen. We are part of God's tapestry, God's unique masterpiece. What a shame if we take it all for granted.

 Notes

Best Friends: Mary Claire Cummins with her gorgeous puppy 'Riley' at their home in Ballinlough, Cork

APRIL 23RD

'The best and safest thing is to keep a balance in your life, acknowledge the great powers around us and in us. If you can do that and live that way, you are a really wise person.' –Euripides

There are always different ways of seeing things in life. We are either optimistic or pessimistic or somewhere in between. The constant message from our Gospels is that there is always a bigger picture. If we take one event in isolation it can give a distorted view. Our world has been around for millions of years and we are a tiny part of the whole story. If we can see the bigger picture, if we can see life from experience, if we can look at it from a faith point of view, if we can look at it from the foundation of good sound values, then life can be viewed with balance. Our prayer today can be a simple one asking God for more balance in every aspect of our lives.

 Notes

Woodland Beauty: A wood at Mount Usher gardens stands out with a carpet of bluebells, near Ashford, Co. Wicklow

APRIL 24TH

'The most basic of all human needs is the need to understand and be understood. The best way to understand people is to listen to them.' ~Ralf Nichols

We might think that we're good at listening but we usually talk far more than we realise. There's a story told about a wise old owl who sat on an oak tree. The more it saw, the less it spoke and the less it spoke, the more it heard. Many people today speak of isolation and alienation. There are many reasons but one is that we are not listening enough to those who are special and important to us. In our Gospels we see how Jesus talked, healed, laughed, loved, challenged, forgave, renewed and most importantly he listened. He allowed each person to share their story. His listening was open, non-judgmental and inclusive. Like the owl we need to speak less and to listen more. It is the greatest gift we can give ourselves and to others.

 Notes

Old And New: A crab apple tree still holds its fruit from last year while new blossoms push forth

APRIL 25TH

'There are too many people praying for mountains of difficulty to be removed, when what they really need is courage to climb them.' ~Author Unknown

We often pray on the spot hoping that a miracle can and will happen. When the spotlight and heat is on, it's the most natural thing for any of us to do. Perhaps if we come at it from a different angle and instead begin to pray for the courage to climb over or through what's difficult. This is a completely different prayer and one that is open and honest. It recognises the need to face the difficulty or challenge head on but it also recognises that it is possible to come through. Our prayer to God today is a prayer asking for courage, not just with mountains of difficulty but courage to face every challenge that we meet in life. For most of us, these challenges hit us often and with the right approach we can be ready for most of them.

 Notes

'I Love You' A mare and foal share an intimate moment with the lovely backdrop of Drishane Castle

APRIL 26TH

'May your roots go down deep into the soil of God's marvellous love. May you have the power to understand as all God's people should, how wide, how long, how high and how deep God's love really is.' ~Ephesians 3:17-18

How would you respond if someone asked are you in love? Would it throw you or would you find it easy to answer? Are we in love with someone, with life, with God? These are key questions but any honest answer can only come from within. Love is a word that is often thrown around wildly and carelessly. It is thrown around so much that we have cheapened its real meaning and value. We hunger for love and we yearn for it. It is the greatest energy in the world but often we search for it in the wrong place. Our prayer today is to acknowledge those who we love and who are so vital and important in our lives. May our roots go down deep into their soil and also into the soil of God's marvellous love for each of us.

 Notes

Orange Ball: The sun dominates the skyline

APRIL 27TH

'One of the greatest mysteries in life is the mystery of time. Everything that happens to us happens in and through time. Time is the force that brings every new experience to the door of your heart.'
~John O'Donoghue

We're all very much aware how time goes by so quickly. We're fast approaching the month of May. April seems to have gone by so quickly. Much of our time and what happens within it is outside our control. But much of it is very much within our sights too, particularly what is happening in the present moment. Nothing is as far away as one minute ago. Nothing is as close as right now. Our faith reminds us how God journeys with us in the right now. Nothing else matters. For all of us the right now is a massive collection of joys, sorrows, pain, happiness, struggles, hopes, fears, weakness, fun, relaxation, anger, freedom, disappointments and so on. We're in there somewhere and so is God.

 Notes

Beach Cycle Path: A cyclist does it the quick way as he cycles across Tramore beach, Co. Waterford

APRIL 28TH

'Give to us a clear vision that we may know where to stand and what to stand for, because unless we stand for something, we shall fall for anything.' ~Peter Marshall

Two buckets met at the well. One of them looked downhearted. "What's the trouble?" asked the second bucket sympathetically. "Oh" replied the first, gloomy bucket, "I get so weary of being dragged to this well. No matter how full I am, I always come back here empty." The second bucket laughed. "How curious!" it chuckled. "Why, I always come here empty and go away full. I'm sure if you started to think this way, you would feel much more cheerful." So many things in life depend on our disposition and what we stand for. We pray to be open to whatever today may bring. We pray for the vision to see more of what's full and promising rather than what's bleak and empty all around us.

 Notes

Climing Into Position: A honeybee climbs on to Arabis flowers

APRIL 29TH

'When we are whom we are called to be, we will set the world ablaze.' ~Catherine of Sienna

Today is the Feast day of St.Catherine and she has been described as one of the most extraordinary figures in Christian history. She preached and acted against the evils of poverty and she preached and acted against corruption in the Church. She only learned to read and write in her adult years and as a lay woman she was an inspiration to all who knew her. So much could be said about Catherine but her constant message was to be yourself, let God touch others through you and use all you have to be a better person in this world. She had great confidence in doing much with the little we have. She described it as setting the world ablaze. What can I do today to set my day ablaze? Catherine would answer it in two simple words: Be yourself.

 Notes

Nice And Cosy!; Trish Macropoulos gets close to St.Fiachra, the patron saint of gardeners, at the Irish National Stud, Co.Kildare

APRIL 30TH

'I can't be happy only on the outside. I have to be happy on the inside too or else I am just presenting a false smile to the world.' ~Michael Buckley

Everyone longs to be happy in some way. We are all searching for it. Many think that money can buy it but not always so. Too often we search for happiness in the wrong places and forget that happiness is often found within us. But unless we are happy with ourselves then we can never find it anywhere else. This becomes the big stumbling block because many find it hard to love themselves within. Why? The world we live in puts huge expectations on us in terms of what we own, what we wear, how we look, what we drive, where we live. No one can live up to these massive expectations. It can leave an empty feeling, even one of failure. In our Gospels Jesus met every person by looking inward and seeing the real person within. Every person he met felt loved to bits. This is real happiness and no money can buy it.

 Notes

MAY

Dazzling Yellow: A field of rapeseed stands out

MAY 1ST

'A life without love is like a year without summer.' ~ Swedish Proverb

Today is 'Lá Bealtaine' which translates as May Day, and today is also the feast of St.Joseph the worker. It's a day that goes way back many generations in Irish culture and history. The day was celebrated to mark the beginning of summer. It was a day when the herds of livestock were driven out to summer pastures. The lighting of bonfires on hills and mountains was a part of the tradition. At the heart of Bealtaine is a reminder of growth, abundance and life flourishing at this time of year. Summer is a season of energy and fulfilment. The darkness of winter is far behind, the promise of spring has delivered and the coming months are about making the most of everything connected with life. Today is a day of great blessing and we ask God to help us make the most of everything connected with life this summer.

 Notes

Between The Rocks: A seal moves gently by

MAY 2ND

'The Spirit of the Lord is upon me because he has anointed me to bring good news to the poor and to give new life to all those in need.' ~Luke 4:18

The word Spirit is mentioned 505 times throughout scripture. Clearly the Spirit of God is hugely important but yet we often don't talk much about it. We feel it's a bit abstract and so best left to one side. A better description is to be found in John's Gospel where the Spirit is called 'The Paraclete'. This translates as 'someone who walks alongside.' We believe the Spirit of God is everywhere but especially that God walks alongside us throughout our lives. This is comforting and consoling. God doesn't happen to be with us occasionally, or abandon us when we do something wrong. God's presence is constant, assured, near and always alongside us. We struggle sometimes to understand how near and close God is. In our joys, struggles, hurts, failures, disappointments, sadness or whatever may be going on for us, God is always there too.

 Notes

Happy As A Pig In ......!!: Scout Eva Twomey wallows in mud as part of the 109th Cork Ballinora Scout Group annual weekend away at Mountmellary Scout Centre

MAY 3RD

'Even though God is the wind beneath your wings, you still have to do a lot of flapping.' ~Brian Cavanaugh

Sometimes people see God as the master magician, who can wave a wand and everything will be as we want. Unfortunately, God does not work that way. The image of God as the wind beneath our wings is a beautiful one. With God on our side we can do so much, we can ride the storms of life, we can have the freedom to go where we want and we can have the confidence to be the person God created each of us to be. But this doesn't just happen and we've got to flap our wings too. We've got to trust. We've got to put our faith and hope into those parts of our lives that we're unsure of. We've got to believe that things can happen. All of this can be summed up in the following prayer: Lord, thank you for being there for me, and together we can and will do so much.

 Notes

Wicklow Hills: Some deer keep a watchful eye as they graze

MAY 4TH

'We prostituted Christianity when we told our people they had to "save their souls". That attitude often affirmed the ego spirituality which is very dangerous and deceptive.' ~*Richard Rohr*

We speak of material consumerism but there is also spiritual consumerism. This is mainly about going through the motions simply for the sake of it. Part of this mindset believes we have to please God by doing certain things. It's almost like a points system and the more points I have, the better chance I have of getting into Heaven. There is absolutely nothing wrong in doing things that please God. But there surely is something wrong if it becomes obligatory, something compulsory and something you have to do. Everything about Jesus in the Gospels is freedom and openness. He extended so many gentle invitations. Some accepted and some ignored. Nobody can say they have it all worked out and no one can say 'tough on those who don't.' The most honest approach is to try and love God in whatever way we can. Whatever way we choose must never be exclusive or cause us to judge others. God will always love us whatever journey or path we choose.

 Notes

'My Space' A spider maximises its opportunity to catch food with this web

MAY 5TH

'We are easily controlled by the voice of our insignificance. This is the illusion that we fall victim to when a small, dark fraction of our lives becomes the whole picture we see of ourselves.' ~Peter Hannah

We are often so hard on ourselves. We are our own worst enemy. We allow something small and insignificant to dominate our lives. Every person has a small fraction of their lives that is dark. We then waste endless time and energy allowing it to dominate our lives. Sometimes it takes over our lives, clouding us in depression, sadness and guilt. We even allow it to blot out God's love for us. We think we are unworthy because we have allowed a pebble become a huge rock in our lives. It's time to go back holding the pebble again and let the rock go. There is great freedom in letting the rock go. There are so many of them in people's lives that need letting go. What is the rock in my life that I need to let go of?

 Notes

Cascading Waterfalls: The River Vartry creates lovely little waterfalls at Mount Usher Gardens in Ashford, Co. Wickow

MAY 6TH

'The greatest thing any of us can do is to be our real self and to live our lives as lovingly and as faithfully as we can and in a way that is pleasing to God.' ~Ronan Scully

Many books have been written about God. There is one obvious link between them all in describing God as love and that this love is very different from human love. God's love is unconditional and it's not based on feelings or emotions. No matter what our standing in life, poor, rich, successful, unsuccessful, struggling, depressed, hopeful, God loves each of us as we are and not as we would like to be. It is we who push up the expectations. We need to be patient and much gentler with ourselves. We need to learn to accept ourselves as we are. God's love for us is beyond our understanding, it is totally genuine and it gives our lives meaning and depth. When in doubt or struggling, hold on to the following words: 'I am unique in God's eyes and nothing will ever change God's total love for me'.

 Notes

Colourful Homes: In Norway every home is built with wood and these colourful homes really stood out in lovely evening sunshine in the village of Flatanger.

MAY 7TH

'Labels are everywhere: gay, goth, skanger, chav, queen, anorexic, retard, geek, clown, druggie, freak, knacker and so on. But what you might regard as harmless stereotyping is actually a practice that can have serious, far reaching and even fatal consequences.' ~Karen Cogan

Labelling, whether positive or negative, is disabling. People have rich and varied personalities. We are indeed unique, complex and made up of a wide variety of beliefs. But we do no favours to ourselves or others when we try to squeeze people into boxes. God never created any of us to be squeezed into categories or labels. We so often make assumptions about someone based on externals, or on what we've heard from other people. This is so limiting and unfair. God created each of us to be free but we often try and limit other people by what we think of them and what we say. Our need to label people often comes from a lack of understanding about a particular group of people. We pray today for a better understanding in how others are trying to live their lives. They too are trying to do their best. Let's give them a fair ch ance.

 Notes

Time To Move On: These dandelion seeds wait for a breeze to take them to new pastures

MAY 8TH

'We need to be aware that drifting off course is almost a certainty. As in sailing; the wind, its direction, force and velocity can easily knock us off course. Our job as followers of Christ is to fight to stay on course.' ~Martin Tierney

The phrase 'drift away' is a nautical one and describes how a boat or ship can drift off course. Even the most experienced sailor is constantly working to counter drifting away. The same is also true of our own lives. There are many things that happen each day that can throw us off course and allow us to drift. Sometimes we might not even be aware we are drifting. It is good to check in with ourselves once in a while. If we are honest with ourselves it's easy to know if we are drifting. Often putting back in place important priorities is a good starting point. Any contact, space or time for God is always one of those priorities. Even a simple honest prayer can be a great starter: "Lord, I feel I am drifting in life. Please help me back on track again".

 Notes

Feeding Time: A foal suckles its mother at the Irish National Stud, Co. Kildare

MAY 9TH

God's Clinic:

I went to God's Clinic to have my routine check-up and it confirmed I was ill. When God took my blood pressure, God saw I was low in tenderness and kindness. Then when God read my temperature it registered 40° of anxiety. An electrocardiogram was then run and it found I needed a love by pass as my arteries were blocked with loneliness and frustration. I was also found to be short-sighted since I could not see beyond the shortcomings of those I live with. When I complained about deafness, the diagnosis was that I had stopped listening to God's voice talking to me on a daily basis. For all that, God gave me a free consultation and gave me some advice. To start with in the morning I'm to take a full glass of gratitude for the day that lies ahead. Later I'm to take a spoon of peace. Every hour I'm to take a pill of patience, a cup of friendship and a glass of humility. Somewhere during the day I'm to take a dose of love and when getting to bed I must take two tablets of clear conscience. When did you last visit God's clinic?

 Notes

Yummy!: Peter Wills enjoying his chocolate cake

MAY 10TH

'Patience, persistence and perspiration make an unbeatable combination for success.' ~Napoleon Hill

There is an old story told about a village that did not have a watchmaker. As the years went by many of the clocks became inaccurate and many of their owners decided to let them run down. But there were others who maintained that as long as the clocks ran, they should not be abandoned. So they wound their clocks day after day even though they knew that they were not accurate. One day news spread through the village that a watchmaker had arrived. Everyone rushed to him with their clocks but the only ones that could be repaired were the ones that had been kept running. The abandoned clocks had grown so full of rust that nothing could be done with them. There are things we do too, that outwardly seem pointless and a waste of time. But in time what might seem foolish and futile now can become precious and special. God always encourages us to patiently persist with small things. With time they always add up to something of much more significance.

 Notes

Sitting Pretty: A fir cone sits steady on a branch with new growth all around it

MAY 11TH

The alphabet of friendship…

A friend Accepts you as you are - Believes in you - Calls you just to say hello – Doesn't give up on you – Envisions the whole of you (even the unfinished parts) – Forgives your mistakes – Gives unconditionally – Helps you – Invites you over – Jokes with you and has a sense of humour – Keeps you close at heart – Loves you for who you are – Makes a difference in your life – Never judges – Offers support – Prays for you – Quietens your fears – Raises your spirits – Says nice things about you – Tells you the truth when you need to hear it – Understands you – Values you – Walks beside you – Xplains things you don't understand – Yells (gently!) when you won't listen – Zaps you back to reality.

 Notes

Waiting Patiently: A swan sits patiently on her eggs in a huge nest

MAY 12TH

There's a story told about a tourist who visited a small village in western Africa.
She saw on her walk around a collection of television sets stacked four deep in a hut at the end
of the village. This same village had received electricity just a few years earlier. No doubt some
manufacturer had presented the people with the essential TVs. But the tourist was obviously
confused by the fact that they were not used and so she went to talk to the village chief. She asked
him, "Why don't your people use the television sets." The chief replied, "We have our storyteller." But
she replied, "Maybe so, but the television has the capacity for thousands of stories." "That's true", said
the chief, "but our storyteller knows us."

Nothing can compete with those who know our story best. The Gospels are a
collection of stories about Jesus. Like the storyteller above, he knows us better
than anyone else. Nothing can replace the intimacy, love and understanding
he brings to all our lives.

 Notes

New Arrivals: A lot can happen in a day and these were the new arrivals

MAY 13TH

'My basic principle is that you don't make decisions because they are easy, you don't make them because they are cheap, you don't make them because they are popular, you make them because they're right.' ~Theodore Hesburg

We make many decisions each and every day. Some are done with effort and ease, some we have to think about and some we find difficult and almost impossible to make. It's the difficult decisions that often throw us. Do we always know when we've made the right decision? From experience we know that at the time it may have seemed right but with hindsight we were proved wrong. But every decision is made in the present moment. Hindsight belongs to the future and is no help. We are free to choose and make our own decisions. Sometimes it calls for great courage. Sometimes it calls for prayer and guidance. We ask God to help us in all our decisions, the small ones and the big ones too.

 Notes

Let The Celebrations Begin: Coláiste Choilm, Ballincollig celebrate after winning the All-Ireland Junior Football Final

MAY 14TH

'A sense of humour doesn't necessarily mean a knack for telling jokes. It means the ability to take some setbacks and still see that the world has not come to an end.' –*Author Unknown*

We all experience setbacks. Some are serious, challenging and can knock us right of our track. Other setbacks are much less serious. When these happen we can just re-adjust and simply move on. We may have complained about little things that didn't go right for us recently. But when such lesser setbacks are put next to other people's real stories and pain, these lesser setbacks fade into total insignificance. Smaller setbacks and knocks are a feature of all our lives. Let's be honest; we're luckier than most and we can count our blessings. We pray today for any person or family who really is experiencing those tough and difficult setbacks in life.

 Notes

On The Edge: A seagull stands on its nest at the edge of a cliff face, at Wicklow Head

MAY 15TH

'There is an inherent good in most difficulties.' ~Norman Peale

Many of the world's finest rugs come from Asia. In many small villages it is a family tradition and all families will work under the direction of a master weaver. They will usually work from the underside of the rug. Sometimes it happens that a weaver absentmindedly makes a mistake and introduces a colour that is not according to the pattern. When this occurs the master weaver, instead of having the work pulled out in order to correct the colour sequence, will always find a way to build the mistake into the overall pattern. It is a lesson we could all hold on to. We too can learn to take our unexpected difficulties and mistakes and weave them to our advantage into the greater pattern of our lives.

 Notes

Colourful Hands: A colourful display in the Church of St.Mary & St.John in Ballincollig as part of
First Holy Communion celebrations

MAY 16TH

'Every action of our lives touches on some chord that will vibrate in eternity.' ~Sean O'Casey

May is the month when everything is vibrating with energy and life. Our gardens are simply bursting with colour. The same can be said of us as well. Every action of ours has an impact and influence that we often don't fully understand or appreciate. Those that are inspired out of love, kindness and goodness are the ones that will always make the biggest impact. They vibrate out to touch and inspire others. Who is my inspiration in life? Who is my biggest influence? Is God an inspiration or influence in my life? This is not always the easiest question to answer. We might need to hold it, along with other important questions in our lives. Every action of ours that has even the tiniest spark of God's influence, will touch and inspire in ways we will never fully understand.

 Notes

We Know We're Just Gorgeous: Three kittens born last month are making great progress

MAY 17TH

The following is a blessing on behalf of the the Chaplaincy/Student Support Team in CIT on our day ahead

May the light of your soul guide you. May the light of your soul bless the work you do with the secret love and warmth of your heart. May you see in what you do, the beauty of your own soul. May the sacredness of your work bring healing light and renewal to those who work with you and to those who see and receive your work. May your work never weary you. May it release within you wellsprings of refreshment, inspiration and excitement. May you be present in what you do. May you never become lost in the bland absences. May the day never burden. May dawn find you awake and alert, approaching your new day with dreams, possibilities and promises. May evening find you gracious and fulfilled. May you go into night blessed, sheltered and protected. May your soul calm, console and renew you.

 Notes

Bursting Forth: Trees at Hollywood, Co. Wicklow are bursting forth with new leaves, flowers and colour

MAY 18TH

'No bit of the natural world is more valuable or more vulnerable than a tree. Nothing is more like ourselves, standing upright, caught between Heaven and Earth, frail at the extremities, yet strong as the central trunk. Nothing is closer to us at the beginning and at the end, providing the timber boards that frame both the cradle and the coffin.' ~*Seamus Heaney*

The image of a tree is a favourite of different writers going back many generations. At the moment many trees are bursting forth with life and energy along with a cascade of green colour. The roots of the tree that go deep into the earth are also symbolic of our own lives. If our roots are shallow and frail we can't expect much in return. But if our roots are deep and strong we can expect much life in return. Our faith and belief in a loving God provide those deep roots that sustain us through life. Time and the experience of generations gone before us have nurtured this belief.

 Notes

Moving On: 6th Years say goodbye to Coláiste Choilm with this beautiful artwork

MAY 19TH

'Wherever you go, no matter what the weather, always bring your own sunshine.' ~Anthony D'Angelo

In nearly every secondary school, Leaving Cert graduation Masses/Services are taking place at the moment. It marks the end of a significant six-year journey and the beginning of a new one. These graduations are hugely significant, meaningful and symbolic. For all the young people involved it is good to look back, reflect and give thanks. For parents it is a huge moment too and the realisation that a son or daughter is about to leave the nest. Unfortunately and unfairly there tends to be a lot of negativity when it comes to young people. This is a great shame. They have endless energy and enthusiasm, they can live in the present moment and they express kindness and love in ways we couldn't even think of. We can be proud of each of them. They face huge challenges too and need our support and love. We congratulate them all and we will keep them very much in our thoughts and prayers.

 Notes

Rolling Hills: The landscape at Newgrange, Co.Meath is particularly eye-catching at this time of year

MAY 20TH

'My best memory from a trip to Africa is of a young man who gave me two of his carvings in exchange for my watch. I got the bargain, he gave me himself, his art and took away a tyrant from my wrist.' ~Richard Rohr

Everyone's perspective and outlook in life is different. The little quotation today is worth reflecting on. It is a reflection on what one side of the world has and what the other doesn't. But it's also a deeper reflection on what is of real and lasting value. The watch is seen as something to be sought-after if you've got nothing, but if you have everything it is referred to as a tyrant. Why? A watch can tie us down, restrict our freedom and be a constant reminder that we must be doing. Or it can be a gentle reminder to live in the present moment, God's most precious gift to you and me today.

 Notes

1, 2, 3, 4 Jump!!!!: These four lads have no fear of heights at Salthill, Galway

MAY 21ST

'If you have a talent, that's God's gift to you. If you use that talent, that's your gift to God.' ~Red Skelton

It's fair to say we take for granted many things in our lives. When we can't do something we begin to realise what we have is important and special. If we were all good at doing the same thing what a boring world we would live in. But what you are good at isn't chance or accident. Very few can do the things you are good at. They can try to imitate you but they will always be only trying. What a shame if we decided not to use our own particular gifts and talents. Using them is our greatest gift in this world and it is also our gift to God. What am I good at doing? What gives me enjoyment and fulfilment? Is there something I am good at but haven't done in a while? Today could be a great day to explore and begin.

 Notes

Yellow Carpet: A racehorse canters through a field of buttercups

MAY 22ND

If you judge people, you have no time to love them. ~Mother Teresa

Two Buddhist monks on their way to the monastery found an exceedingly beautiful woman at the river bank. Like them, she wished to cross the river, but the water was too high. So one of the monks lifted her on his back and carried her across. The fellow monk was thoroughly scandalized. For two full hours he berated him on his negligence in keeping the holy rule: Had he forgotten that he was a monk? How dare he chat her up and actually carry her across the river? And what would people say? Had he not brought their holy religion into disrepute? The offending monk patiently listened to the never-ending sermon. Finally, he broke in with, "Brother, I dropped the woman at the river. Are you still carrying her?"

 Notes

My Resting Place: A spider finds its own place to rest

MAY 23RD

'The wall which prevents us from seeing God is our concept of God. We miss God because we think we know. That is the terrible thing about religion.' ~Anthony DeMello

Many of us think we know a lot about everything. If we're really honest, there is so little we know. We discover more and more about our world and our lives with each passing day. We will never be able to say at any stage that we know it all. This is especially true of God and who we think God is or might be. No religion can give you the whole package and say 'this is what it's all about'. Every day is our gift from God to use it as best we can. Each day we can discover God in the heartbeat of life, at home, at work, at church, at school, on the training pitch, in our garden, in our local shop, everywhere and anywhere. We can never know everything about God but one thing we know with absolute certainty; God is closer to us than we can possibly imagine.

 Notes

Going For A Quick Dip: Laura O'Donoghue from Coláiste Choilm about to plunge under one of the waterfalls that run into the Silver River near Cadamstown, Co.Offaly

MAY 24TH

'If you do not know how to recognise your own faults, have recourse to true, faithful friends and they will tell you. They are above all your own conscience and the angels of God. Get to know them, become familiar with them.' ~Pierre Favre

We all have our faults with no exception. The only problem is that we tend to point out the faults in others much easier instead of beginning with ourselves. It's not just you or me, it seems to be a human trait in all of us. Some of our faults are so inbuilt we can do little with them. But many we can tweak, change and adjust to make life better for ourselves and for others too. That's when a good friend can be such a blessing, pointing out where we are weak and importantly helping us find a way forward in a positive way. We thank God also today for our friends, particularly those who are faithful, loyal and always there for us.

 Notes

May Colour: A fly finds the shade on the leaf of a Dove tree

MAY 25TH

'Wrong is wrong, even if everyone is doing it. Right is right, even if no one is doing it.' – Author Unknown

Sin seems to be a word that has lost its way in the world. It seems to be no longer popular, has no roots and seems to be homeless. There are many reasons why we have lost our sense of sin. We all know that there was a huge negative emphasis on sin for many generations. It choked our sense of good and of God's love for us. People were made feel guilty, they felt a deep sense of shame and felt worthless? What a far cry from how God understands each of us, how fragile we are and yet how strong we can be too. If sin is a word that is no longer cool, then what words are appropriate? Perhaps Gandhi's few words sum it up best, "God hates the sin but loves the sinner." What have I done wrong in recent times? How can I put things right? Can I ask God for forgiveness? God's gentle words to each of us will always be: "You are forgiven – now go in peace."

 Notes

Laughter The Best Medicine: A chimpanzee sees the funny side of life in Dublin Zoo

MAY 26TH

'Human life is a journey. Life is like a voyage on the sea of history, often dark and stormy, a voyage in which we watch for the stars to indicate the route. The true stars of our lives are the people close by us and who guide us along the way.' ~Pope Benedict XVI

The month of May is traditionally dedicated to Mary. She is sometimes referred to as the 'Star of the Sea'. Considering the dangers of sea travel in ancient times, it is easy to imagine that sailors and passengers prayed to Mary for protection and a safe journey. The image of Mary as Star of the Sea became popular as the years went on. Jesus has also been referred to as a star, particularly the Northern Star. It is the brightest star in the sky, is constant and never moves. It is good to have a star to guide and direct us in life. Who is the star in your life that guides and directs you? As we journey through this final week of May, we might keep Mary in mind as a star in our lives.

 Notes

Minutes Old: Lucinda, an Anglo Nubian goat begins the bonding process with her new arrivals

MAY 27TH

'Every time we say, "I believe in the Holy Spirit," we mean that we believe that there is a living God able and willing to enter human personality and change it.' ~JB Philips

How does one describe the Holy Spirit? We have all been in a restaurant where the waitress has asked, "Can I warm up your coffee for you?" The cup may be half full and cold after sitting on the table for a while. When she pours the new coffee in, she refills and warms up the whole cup once again. In ways, we are like the cup of coffee as well, perhaps we are spiritually cold and empty. We need a spiritual boost. God willingly wants to fill each of us with the Holy Spirit, to renew and refresh, to instil hope and to impart life in each of us. We ask the Holy Spirit to guide and direct us and to teach us what's really important in life. Why not pause for a brief moment and pray quietly to the Holy Spirit for guidance and direction.

 Notes

Feeding Time A wagtail feeds its young with an insect while the others scream for their portion. Photo was captured using a hidden camera over the nest worked by remote control to minimise disturbance.

MAY 28TH

'For everything there is a season, a time for meeting, a time to say goodbye. For everything there is a season, a time for loving, a time for letting go. In all things God is near, always guiding your way.'
~Celtic Blessing

At the heart of Celtic spirituality is the idea that God is close and near. It embraces life and that everything works in cycles. There is a time and a place for all that needs to be done. Everything that lives and breathes is a reflection on the beauty of God. Such a spirituality is simple with a no-nonsense approach. It is uplifting and to the point. It is close to people and nature. It is we who tend to over-complicate matters when it comes to following God. An over-emphasis on rules and regulations have often stifled areas of growth. No wonder Jesus attacked the Scribes and Pharisees for their negativity. Today I can be open to God's gentle presence in my life, not distant or removed but instead close, near and guiding me through this day.

 Notes

Lunchtime: A seagull feasts on a lobster at Portmagee, Co.Kerry

MAY 29TH

Which is better to have – a clock that gains twenty seconds each day or the one that does not work at all?

Answer: The clock that is broken will be the better of the two. Although it does not work, this clock will show the correct time twice each day. The clock that gains twenty seconds every day is right only once every five years and 328 days. Every single one of us has our weaker points, limitations, faults and mistakes. Some of these we are encouraged to let go of and some we have to live with. Like a broken clock that tells the correct time each day our weaker points can also be points of growth and strength. Even when we get it wrong God always wants to point us in the right direction. We are never condemned, judged or made feel guilty. Others may try, but never God.

 Notes

'Best Friends' Kim Broderick relaxes near Coláiste Choilm, Ballincollig, with the summer holidays about to begin

MAY 30TH

'Awareness is noticing the blessings that often get overlooked in our busy lives. Gratitude for a special blessing can inspire us to look further and discover even more good in our lives. As we are inspired, let us also be inspiring to others.' ~Author Unknown

If we tend to see today as the same as any other day, then we have lost our sense of awareness. Yes there is a lot of repetition from day to day in many of the things we do, but the blessings that today will bring will never be the same as the ones you had yesterday, and tomorrow is an entirely different story. Busy lives and heavy working schedules put on the blinkers and our awareness of these blessings. Can we pause when a special moment happens? Can we hold it? Can we allow it to inspire us? Every inspiring moment has its roots in God.

 Notes

Rock Solid Foundation: The world famous Fastnett Rock looking splendid off the West Cork coastline

MAY 31ST

'We can feel the rush of warmth and kindness, the sudden urgency of love that sent that girl hurrying over the hills.' ~Caryll Houselander

Today is the Feast of the Visitation when Mary made the journey to visit her cousin Elizabeth. Both were pregnant and we're told that when they met, the child in Elizabeth's womb leaped for joy. We don't have a journalistic account of their meeting but we do have a poetic account of their encounter. Mary expresses beautiful words of praise to God for all that was happening in her life. These words have been put together to form the beautiful prayer called 'The Magnificat'. We might say the story has no relevance for us and yet it has much to say as well. Mary and Elizabeth made quality time for each other, shared their innermost feelings, their joys, their worries, struggles, hopes and fears. They were more than just cousins and treasured each other's friendship. Do I take for granted or do I really treasure my best friends?

 Notes

JUNE

Out It Pops: Silage making in full swing

JUNE 1ST

'Spring being a tough act to follow, God created June.' ~Al Bernstein

It is hard to believe that today is the first day of June. Did you know that no other month in the year begins on the same day as 1st June? It is a much anticipated month, with schools getting holidays, nature bubbling with life and colour, father's day is celebrated and the feast of St.John is celebrated on June 24th. June is a time of year when everything peaks with maximum daylight hours. The pearl is the birthstone for the month of June. It is a symbol of purity and because they are so rare they are considered gems. Spiritually they are a reminder that we are all pearls in God's eyes, precious and uniquely special. As we begin our journey through June today we ask God's many blessings on each of us. We pray that this month will be fruitful, healthy and life giving for us. We include anyone who has asked us to pray for them, particularly those starting the Junior and Leaving Cert exams. May every day of the coming 30 of this month be a day when you feel God close and near to you.

 Notes

Perfect Formation: The Red Arrows look spectacular as they loop in perfect formation

JUNE 2ND

'We who live in prison, have to measure time by throbs of pain and the record of bitter memories.'
~Oscar Wilde

The film 'The Shawshank Redemption' did well when it came out first. But its spectacular success has come in the years since. It is one of the most popular rented DVD and sales of the film have been consistent over a long period of time. It's a story of hope against all the odds. It's about people in jail and having the hope to get out. Why does this film have such universal appeal? It's not because everyone has been to jail. But on a deeper level many people feel at times that they are. They feel enslaved and trapped in their own lives, in their work situations, in their lack of work, in relationships, families or whatever puts walls and bars around us. The Shawshank Redemption is a story about escaping from that imprisonment. God also wants to free us from whatever our prison might be. God wants to unlock those gates, bring us out and throw the keys away. Whatever our prison might be, can I invite God in and help me to a better place in my life?

 Notes

No Fear: Cooling down at the weir in Ballincollig Regional Park

JUNE 3RD

A short prayer for those starting exams…..

Loving God, I turn to you today. As the exam approaches I am nervous and so I ask you to help me. You know how important these exams are to me. Set me free from worry, give me your peace and help me to think clearly. Help me to remember what I have learned, to use my time well, not to panic, to do my best and not to worry about the outcome. Help me to realise that the exams are not there to catch me out but to find out how much I know. Lord, keep me calm so that I can write down all I know! Keep my friends calm too, we're all in this together. Let me sleep each night so that I am refreshed and renewed for the next exam. Even if I struggle I must always remember that there is a bigger picture of which these exams are only a small part of. Most important of all calm me down, keep me focussed, guide me along, get me through the scary moments and make sure I attempt every question. Thank you for being my friend today and always. Amen.

 Notes

Cottage Garden Kitchen Rose: A stunning rose reminding us of the vibrant colours that June can bring.

JUNE 4TH

'It can be a long human trek to the heart. How hard many of us find it to get in touch, with how we really feel deep down. Whole lives can be lived and wasted without once knowing how they feel. Whole life spans can be spent without ever having truly lived.' ~*Joe Armstrong*

Different parts of the world vary but in the western world we are totally focussed on the externals. We sweep along with a daily run of non-stop events. The pace is usually hectic and it leaves little space for quiet time or reflection. We seldom look within or take the time to check in on how we are genuinely feeling. Men (and I include myself here) are the worst culprits. When asked how do we feel the response is normally, "Fine", "Grand", "Sound". It's an invisible wall we put up and it needs to be knocked. There is a huge need to bring some balance back in and to spend some little time being honest with our innermost feelings. It's an area of our lives that is so overlooked and neglected. It's time to journey inward. A little, done consistently over time, would make such a difference.

 Notes

Mountain Top Views: The views from Clara mountain looking across at Millstreet, Co.Cork

JUNE 5TH

'If you want to build a ship, don't herd people together to collect wood and don't assign them tasks and work, but rather teach them to long for the endless immensity of the sea.' ~*Antoine de Saint-Exupéry*

One certainty in life is that we will never fully understand God. We can never describe God from A to Z. It's a lifetime challenge. But we do have endless pointers on the journey of life that remind us of God's unique presence in our world and universe. Some of these describe God as love, as our creator, who is generous, who is with us always, who forgives wholeheartedly, who delights in each of us, who trusts us, encourages us, watches over us, comforts us and someone who brings light and hope to our dark corners. There are thousands of more words that could be added and we would still be short. In trying to understand God we must always remember God's endless love for each of us. Everything else evolves from this.

 Notes

Gotcha: A spider closes in on a fly trapped in its web

JUNE 6TH

'This is what the world wants from the Church, not sermons, not words, but to live in such a way that Christian qualities can be seen in the way we live our lives.' –The Universe

There is a story told about a young Armenian nurse working in a hospital in the Middle East. A Turkish man was brought into her ward and placed under her care. She recognised him as the one who had killed her father and mother. He also recognised her. The man lived in constant fear, waiting for the revenge he was sure would come. At mealtimes, he expected a lethal dose of poison in his food. At night, he listened for the slightest sound, expecting the thrust of a dagger in his back. Nothing of the sort happened. Day and night the young nurse cared for him, pleasantly and patiently as if he were her brother. Finally the man could stand it not longer. He said to the nurse: "You know who I am. Why do you treat me with such kindness?" The nurse replied: "I am a Christian, Christ has taught us to love our enemies." He answered: "I never knew there was a religion like that."

 Notes

Circle Of Smiles: Sarah O'Connell with Lili Shepherd, Máiréad, Eabha, Culann and Emily McNally

JUNE 7TH

A friendship blessing by the late John O'Donohue

May you be blessed with good friends. May you learn to be a good friend to yourself. May you be able to journey to that place in your soul where there is great love, warmth, feeling and forgiveness. May this change you. May it transfigure that which is negative, distant or cold in you. May you be brought into real passion, kinship and affinity of belonging. May you treasure your friends. May you be good to them and may you be there for them. May they bring you all the blessings, challenges, truth and light that you need for your journey. May you never be isolated and may you always be in the gentle nest of belonging with your anam cara.

 Notes

Church Views: The Church of the Immaculate Conception in Clonakilty looks well in summer sunshine

JUNE 8TH

'I must reflect that there are other people who would somehow remain peaceful, optimistic, gentle and unruffled if they were in my shoes at this time.' ~John Powell

We all react in different ways to different situations. We sometimes get it wrong, we over-react and we put ourselves under unnecessary pressure. We often think we are dealing with it the right way, but sometimes what we think is right may not always be the best way. It is quite true that someone else might do things differently if they were in our shoes. They may also get it wrong. Most of the time we do just fine and we handle situations as best we can. But if we tend to over-react, get worried, anxious or stressed over lots of small things in our life, then we need to be much gentler with ourselves. How would Jesus react if he were in our shoes? He probably would remain calm, optimistic, peaceful, compassionate, understanding and helpful. He would be honest, challenging and upfront too. But most importantly we would know that he was on our side. Can I be the same for anyone in my life?

 Notes

Cooling Down: A baby elephant named Asha gets a nice cool shower at Dublin Zoo

JUNE 9TH

'To describe something, to simply name something properly, in some way already sets you above it. To name something is not to be fully imprisoned by it.' ~Ronald Ronheiser

It is good to name something, be upfront and then deal with it. It is often tempting to tip-toe around something without actually naming it. We do so in case we upset or offend, but we also do it to avoid something we don't want to face up to. What sort of stuff do we avoid naming? Examples could include any form of addiction, feeling depressed, feeling suicidal, pressures at home or in work, pressure within a relationship or a mistake made. Once we name something it is out in the open and it gives us the freedom to do something about it. When it's not named, we tend to be in denial and never give ourselves the chance to move on. In many of our Gospel stories Jesus often asked, "What do you want me to do for you?" He gave each person the opportunity to name it and then he helped them into a much better place. Can I name something I have been avoiding?

 Notes

Cuckoo Spit: They are to be found on many plants and flowers at this time of year

JUNE 10TH

'Though religion claims more believers than ever, it has seldom wielded so little influence on public life. Now we compete tooth and claw for the new values our civilisation holds most dear.' ~*Michael Farrell*

These values do tend to change and particularly during an economic downturn. A few years ago some of these values could have been named as wealth, dominance, prosperity, celebrity status, control and the notion that 'I can have more and I can have nearly everything I want'. These values in recent times have got a right old knock and have been shaken to the core. Rightly or wrongly these values will always be around but there is a noticeable shift. We now realise that we can't have everything, that there are limits and that new values need to be nurtured. So what might these be? A sense of fairness, equality and balance. A sense of humility and openness. A sense of community and togetherness. A sense of feet firmly on the ground and taking it one step at a time. A sense of spirituality, sacredness, mystery and that there is a bigger picture of which God is a central part. I'm sure you could add more.

 Notes

I Love You: Maxi one of the most affectionate dogs known, gives Aoife McSweeney a big sloppy kiss

JUNE 11TH

The following reflection called 'Please Hear What I'm Not Saying' gives us food for thought:

Don't be fooled by me. Don't be fooled by the face I wear. For I wear a mask, a thousand masks, masks that I'm afraid to take off and none of them is me. Pretending is second nature to me but don't be fooled. I give you the impression that I'm secure, that confidence is my name and coolness is my game. But don't believe me. My surface may seem smooth but my surface is my mask, ever-varying and ever concealing. Beneath lies confusion, fear and aloneness. But I hide this. I don't want anybody to know it. My only hope is acceptance if it's followed by love. It's the only thing that can liberate me from myself. You have got to help me. You've got to hold out your hand even when that's the last thing I seem to want. Only you can call me into aliveness. Each time you're kind, gentle and encouraging. Each time you try to understand, you can breathe life into me. Who am I you may wonder? I am someone you know very well. I am every man and woman you meet each day.

 Notes

My Own World: A fisherman waits patiently in the River Lee, near Ballincollig, Co.Cork

JUNE 12TH

'Divine Providence is a conspiracy of accidents through which God speaks.' ~James Mackey

Do you believe in Divine Providence? Or do you see it as a random act of pure luck that happens to come your way? For each person the answer is personal. If God is a part of your life and even if at times this connection is haphazard or distant, we can still be sure that Divine Providence is never too far away. The Bible is a collection of books telling us about God's finger inside many different events over a long period of time. The task of faith is to try and understand what God is saying, not just in these events but in our own personal lives and events too. In understanding Divine Providence, God is not a magician. God can't prevent random acts from happening and God doesn't answer every prayer with a yes. Divine Providence assures us that there is something more to life as we know it. It also assures us that somehow in this crazy complex world that we live in, there is meaning, fulfillment and a purpose to everything we do.

 Notes

Fireball: A stunt bike rider rides high into the flames at Curaheen Park, Bishopstown

JUNE 13TH

'The great crisis of Christian faith in Europe and elsewhere is not the lack of vocations or the scandals or the very real lack of financial resources. The great crisis is that the Church, all of us who are Baptised, has lost its hunger for the living God' ~Seamus O'Connell

There is no denying that the Church is in crisis, not a small one but of colossal proportions. For many years when a crack appeared, it was covered up without asking the fundamental question; is there subsidence? We know today that the Church has indeed major subsidence. Builders tackle subsidence by pumping the strongest of concrete into the foundations. Then all the cracks and external damage can be dealt with. What are we going to pump into the foundations of the Church of which we are all a part of in some way? There is a need to get back to the simple basics and renew a hunger for our living God. As we rebuild and restart there has to be openness, inclusion and honesty. Let's invite God back in again and then start building. It can't be a few here and a few there. It has to be everyone building together.

 Notes

A Safe Landing: Olé Martin is a modern day St.Francis. Seagulls and many forms of wildlife know his every move in the village of Flatanger, north west Norway

JUNE 14TH

'The foundations for a better tomorrow must be laid today' ~Author Unknown

The image of a foundation is one that is often used to explain the important things in our lives which give deep meaning and value. In our Gospels, Jesus uses the image of building on rock or sand. A house built on rock can withstand any flood whereas the one built on sand will collapse. A poor foundation may be the result of a geological fault where the earth collapses underneath, it may be due to poor materials or poor construction. We too are challenged to look at the foundations of our own lives. There is much goodness, trust and love in many of our foundations. We need to hold all of these and much more. It is good news and makes you who you are. The poor foundations are areas in all of our lives that need improving. For every one of us this area is going to be different. Every poor foundation can be strengthed into something positive and worthwhile.

 Notes

Spoilt For Choice: A honey bee is busy collecting nectar

JUNE 15TH

'I am thankful to be given the chance to perhaps be in the right place at the right time and so be a light in the life of a few.' ~Róisín Hall

How often have we heard someone say that they were in the wrong place at the wrong time. If only the clock could be turned back to change things, but sadly it can't. Just as the clock can't turn back, neither can it be pushed forward and that leaves us with today. This day is made up of many significant moments. Thankfully we can choose to be in the right place at the right time for someone in our lives today. It need not be earth-shattering and it need not cost the world. God is often most active and alive in the simplest, down-to-earth moments of our daily lives. Any gesture done with love means we are always in the right place at the right time.

 Notes

Gorse And Heather: A lovely combination of yellow and purple transform the Connemara landscape

JUNE 16TH

'Dig within. Within is the wellspring of good and it is always ready to bubble up, if you just dig.'
~Marcus Aurelius

We so often put the emphasis on the externals, stuff to get done, deadlines to meet, shopping to be done, bills to be paid and so much more. Much of this stuff is important and most of it has to be done. But in all the doing we think everything else is unimportant. But within each person is a vast treasure or wellspring of goodness and love bubbling up. It needs expression but only if we allow it. At the heart of our belief system is to give expression to what is important within. No person can ever take that away from us no matter how hard they try. The image of something bubbling up has always been associated with the Divine. We can ask God to allow us to bubble over with love, goodness and so many more blessings.

 Notes

You're Not Getting Away!: A seagull is determined that this fish will not leave its firm grasp

JUNE 17TH

'I am only one, but I am one. I cannot do everything, but I can do something. And I will not let what I cannot do interfere with what I can do.' ~Edward Everett Hale

'World Blood Donor Week' is always marked during the month of June. Millions of people around the world owe their lives to individuals they will never meet. These are the people who donate their blood to help others. It is important to raise awareness about the need for more support. Here in Ireland 3,000 donations are needed each week. Only 3% of the Irish population are donors providing blood for a population of four million. One in four people will need a transfusion at some point in their lives. We often say, "Sure, it won't be me", "I'll be grand", "I'm fine and healthy". But life as we know is fragile and the unexpected is something we can't avoid. A single donation of blood can save up to three lives. Blood is our lifeline. It's precious and sacred and we thank God for it. We can give the gift of life to someone else. It is the most precious gift we can give.

 Notes

Scenic Harbour: Caherciveen harbour in Co.Kerry is a hive of activity, particularly during the summer months

JUNE 18TH

'Every time you smile at someone, it is an action of love, a gift to that person, a beautiful thing.'
—Mother Teresa

A smile may seem small and almost insignificant and yet its impact can last a lifetime. We all know a genuine smile when we see it, radiating the inner beauty of the person within. Sadly we don't seem to be smiling as much today. One can call it busyness, worry or stress but it seems we have forgotten the power of a smile. Maybe forgotten is the wrong word but we certainly need to smile more. We need to allow the simplicity and beauty of a smile to express the Divine within. We need to allow it to touch others and neverto underestimate its beauty. Even when we're stuck for words in the great mystery of life, from joy to great sadness, a smile can often be better than a thousand words.

 Notes

Divided Loyalties: Sisters Caitríona and Órla Ní Chathasaigh have the final say in who will triumph between Cork and Kerry in the football championship

JUNE 19TH

'Life's battles don't always go to the stronger or fastest person. But sooner or later, the person who wins is the one who thinks they can.' ~Author Unknown

Every single one of us faces those ongoing life battles. Life is fragile and its sharp edges touch everyone at some stage. We sometimes think that others have the edge on us but they don't really. If we think we are beaten in life then we most certainly are. But if we are willing to face everything with some courage and determination we will pull through. Equally we may have to reach out and help somebody else who thinks they are beaten. It can so easily happen with a lack of self confidence, a bout of depression or just overwhelmed by what lies ahead. We can be the one who can gently give them the confidence to take that all important step forward.

 Notes

Eagle Precision: A White Tailed Eagle swoops for a fish at lightning speed just off the coast of Flatanger, north west Norway

JUNE 20TH

'Everything can be taken from us except one thing, the last of human freedoms – to choose one's own attitude in any given set of circumstances' ~Viktor Frankl

Viktor Frankl was No. 119,104 in a concentration camp during the Second World War. He worked many hours alone and with no escape, he was helpless. In such a miserable situation many of us would wilt into utter misery but he always kept a positive spirit. He only focussed on thoughts that empowered him and always took great comfort from the beauty of nature around him. Each of us too has the freedom to choose our own attitude in life and in any given situation. No matter how powerless we may be, we can turn any positive or chink of light available to our advantage.

 Notes

Midsummer Sunset: A midsummer sunset marks the longest day of the year with 17 hours, 1 minute and 26 seconds of sunshine today

JUNE 21ST

'Some things occur only in darkness, the sprouting of a seed, the development of an unborn child, the bustle of nocturnal animals and insects. We humans know the beauty of eating by candlelight, sitting around a campfire, praying in an unlit chapel or making love in the darkness.'
~Melannie Svoboda

Today is Midsummer's Day. Darkness will be limited to just a few hours tonight. We are sometimes afraid and fear the dark. This is not something new. It stretches back thousands of years. It is true that God loves light but it's also true that God loves darkness as well. In the book of Exodus we are told that the people stood at a distance while Moses drew near to the darkness where God was. Life is a mixture of light and darkness for all of us. We flourish and thrive when we are in the light and we often struggle in the dark. But from God's point of view, God is with us in light but also in darkness too. So no matter how dark, sad, dreary or depressing our lives may be at times, our heart-felt belief is that somehow God is present in there as well.

 Notes

Colourful Meadow: A bull calf takes it nice and easy in a meadow of buttercups

JUNE 22ND

'I need all my energy for living towards your fullness. The energy I expend in anger and resentment is diverted and lost. The energy I use for loving and praying is multiplied.' ~Margaret Silf

Some people seem to be naturally bubbly and full of energy, more have far less, and for many we fluctuate somewhere in between. It makes sense to conserve and use wisely what we have. It's been well documented how anger, resentment, jealousy and hatred simply eat up much of our energy reserves. Over a long period of time it can leave us feeling totally exhausted. Any time we love, pray and reach out in God's name, not only saves our energy levels but multiplies them many times over. Throughout this day I can make an effort to use my energy for living life to the full. We know what doesn't work, we know what does, and the choice will always be mine.

 Notes

Bonfire Night: A bonfire blazes near Wilton, Cork on the eve of the Feast of John the Baptist

JUNE 23RD

The following is a powerful reflection and was found in Reality magazine.
We carry so many unnecessary burdens with us each day. What can I let go of today?

Let go of the desire to control. Let go of anger. Let go of shame. Let go of guilt. Let go of worries. Let go and let things follow their natural course. Let go of the need to use every second to the full. Let go of fear. Let go of tension. Let go of the need to be right. Let go of the need to be successful. Let go of the need to seem strong or know it all. Let go of the future you had charted out for yourself. Let go of the need to be the best. Let go of self rejection. Let go of the impulse to do more than can reasonably be done in the time available. Let go of regrets and disappointments. Let go of trying to change others. Let go of criticism. Let go of being harsh on yourselves and others. Let go of prejudices and biases. Let go of interfering.

 Notes

Summer Smiles: Aisling and Emer Gleeson are all smiles at the Midsummer Festival in Fitzgerald's Park, Cork

JUNE 24TH

'Learn to use things and love people, rather than using people and loving things.' ~Author Unknown

Today we celebrate the Feast of John the Baptist. He was a celebrity in his own way. Thousands flocked to hear him and be baptised by him. But John was not interested in fame. He never wanted to draw attention to himself. John's mission was to prepare the way for Jesus. He was a bit like a groundsman before an important game. He lined the pitch, mowed the grass just right and got everything ready as it should be. Then when the game started he stepped back, knowing his job was done. He wanted to draw attention only to Jesus. Sometimes we hang our heads and often we're not proud of what we believe in. It's almost as if it is unfashionable and a bit embarrassing to say we believe. John was the exact opposite. He had no reservations and no inhibitions in proclaiming that he was proud to be a follower of Jesus. We too are called to hold our heads up. We are called to be proud of what we believe and to be grateful that we have indeed something to build our lives on.

 Notes

Jagged Coastline: The west Cork coastline has a unique beauty near Rosscarbery

JUNE 25TH

'You cannot pull people uphill who do not want to go, you can only point up.' ~Amy Carmichael

Not everyone agrees with our viewpoints or our approach to certain things. We would like everyone to go with our own ideas but people do have different and varied viewpoints that need to be respected. We can only put forward our own viewpoint or ideas. We can't force them on anyone. In our Gospels Jesus never forced his message on anyone and always respected different viewpoints. Unfortunately, a close look at Church history will point to the exact opposite. The emphasis was often on fear and punishment. Thankfully the emphasis today is on inclusiveness and respect. It can only begin with ourselves. We can be proud of what we believe in, we can share it with others, we may be enthusiastic or lukewarm about it, but we can never force it on anyone.

 Notes

Nightime Skyline: A beautiful skyline taken at midnight looking through a tree, gives the picture a whole new depth of beauty just off the north west coast of Norway

JUNE 26TH

'Can an artist ever have enough brushes? The longer I paint, the more convinced I am that brushes get better as they get older, until some are really too worn down to be of any use.' ~David Millard

We live in a disposable world. Everything seems to have such a short life span from instant food to fast food, from every sort of a convenient gadget to the latest invention, a toothbrush that you can chew as you go! But some things do get better with age and time. Wine is an obvious example and even paint brushes do well with age. The same applies to many Christian values such as love, kindness, forgiveness, healing, openness and honesty. These can never be disposed, they have held their value over time and will continue to do so for many more years. If we just take even one important value, what is it for you? Is it something you can hold close to you, knowing that the longer you hold it, the better you become as a person.

 Notes

Jumping Clear: A hedge in the shape of a horse and rider is particulary eyecatching on a roundabout near the Curragh racecourse, Co.Kildare

JUNE 27TH

'Today those who wish to preach the gospel need to connect with their audience, speaking to them in their own language and connecting with their hopes and fears, their aspirations and disappointments.' ~Francis Cousins

If you were to do a review of the last 25 years how, would you sum it up? It has been a constant evolution of changes. The biggest change has been the digital revolution and how technology has progressed at an incredible pace. From a spiritual point of view we also have to adapt to the progress all around us. Some would say is it really progress? But such an attitude will simply leave us watching from the sidelines with many opportunities slipping us by. The Gospel message will always be the same, fresh, energetic and uplifting. The challenge is to connect it to people's lives by using every modern means of communication. There is still room for tradition and bringing forward many things that worked well for us in the past. But only if we're open to exploring new methods of evangelisation.

 Notes

Beautiful Coastline: The views looking across at Galley Head Lighthouse, near Rosscarbery, west Cork

JUNE 28TH

A young girl said to her friend, "When I get older, I want to wear glasses just like Granny's because she can see so much more than most people. She can see the good in a person when everyone else sees a bad side. She can see what a person meant to do even if they didn't do it. I asked her one day how she could see the good and she said it was the way she learned to look at things as she got older. When I get older, I want to wear a pair of glasses just like Granny's so I can see the good too."
~Walter Buchanan

What a different world we could live in if we all wore a pair of Granny's glasses! Why is there such emphasis on the negative? Why do we allow it to dominate our lives? There is such a vast reservoir of goodness out there. We don't have to wear special glasses but we do need a certain mindset. Our prayer today might be to ask God to help us see some good around us even if it's hard to find.

 Notes

Summer Colour: Our gardens are alive with all sorts of vibrant colours at this time of year

JUNE 29TH

'Any person who knows all the answers most likely misunderstood the questions in the first place.'
~Author Unknown

It would be great if we had all the answers. Every single one of us has so many unanswered questions. Life can be so unpredictable, unfair and cruel at times. What did I do to deserve this? Why me? Why not somebody else? Why now? It's easy to blame somebody else or to blame God. This is understandable. It becomes unhealthy when we're stuck in blame and never move on with our lives. Today we celebrate the Feast of St.Peter and St.Paul. Their lives were marked by courage, conviction and enthusiasm. But they too had their struggles, and questions. Even at times their deep faith left them short. The invitation is to live the questions and with time we may get glimpses of an answer. Sometimes the unanswered bits and pieces pull together when we least expect. We pray today for the strength to live with all our questions and the strength to walk forward with our lives, even if it's only small, faltering steps.

 Notes

Climbing On Up: A fly makes its way to the top of a leaf

JUNE 30TH

It was the last day before the summer holidays and the children brought presents for their teacher who they wouldn't see again. As it was the last day the teacher decided to make a game of guessing what the presents were. First the shop owner's daughter came with a box. It was heavy. "Is this a box of sweets?" "Yes" replied the little girl. Next the flower shop owner's son came up with a box. It was light. So the teacher shakes it and says, "Are these flowers?" "Yes" said the little boy. Next came the wine merchant's daughter with a box. It's very heavy. The teacher shakes it and it leaks. The teacher touches the liquid with her finger and tastes it and says, "Is this box full of wine?" "No Miss", came the reply. The teacher tastes another drop and says "Is it a bottle of champagne?" "No Miss" comes the reply again. "I give up" the teacher says. "Tell me what's in the box?" "A puppy" the little girl says!

It's good to have a sense of humour. It is God's gift to us, enabling us to smile or laugh.

 Notes

JULY

Colourful Butterfly: A butterfly looks for nectar on a flower

JULY 1ST

'In a world that is changing daily before our very eyes and often it seems unpleasantly so, it is comforting to have certainties to hold onto.' ~*Mary Murphy*

We like to be certain about most things. It is no surprise that we sometimes say: "As sure as I'm standing here", or "As sure as night follows day", or "As sure as I woke up this morning". We are relaxed and comfortable with ourselves when we're in a place with certainty, where one and one make two, when the month of June rolls into July as it has done today and when we know the right answer to a question. We're not so relaxed when we're wrong or when we make a mistake. To hold one's hand up and say 'I got it wrong' is honest, truthful, and apologetic but it can also leave us vulnerable. We're not always welcoming of those who say 'I got it wrong'. Often our first reaction is to say, 'Told you so'. What's the point in trying to get one up on someone? The Christian response is to be supportive, to forgive and to help the person move on with their lives.

 Notes

Double Cry: These two-day old swallow chicks are in full voice in an outhouse

JULY 2ND

A Relationship Creed...

You and I are in a relationship which is so important to me and I want it to be important to you too. Each of us is a unique person with separate needs. You have the right to meet your needs and I have the right to meet mine. Also, we have the right to our own beliefs and values. I will respect your rights and I want you to respect mine. When my actions interfere with your needs, I want you to tell me, I will then listen and change if I can. When either of us cannot change to meet the other's needs, let's face our conflict and solve it together. I don't want to lose by letting you win and I don't want to win by making you lose. I want to find solutions that are acceptable to both of us so that we can both win. By following this creed our relationship has every chance of growing. It can with your help, with God's help and by journeying every step together.

 Notes

Nice And Easy: Tourists enjoying the views along the Gap Of Dunloe, near Killarney

JULY 3RD

'What makes a river so restful to people is that it doesn't have any doubt. It is sure to get where it is going and it doesn't want to go anywhere else.' ~Hal Boyle

Few of us are as confident as a river. It may have twists and turns, it sometimes may be in flood but for the most part it journeys on at its own pace, seemingly unaffected by what's going on all around it. If only we could be unaffected by what's going on all around us. But we're not because it is part of our human nature to be sensitive. Today is the Feast of St.Thomas. He also was sensitive and he had his doubts. But yet he has been branded the "Doubting Thomas" as if what he did and said was wrong. But he should be praised for his honesty, openness and courage to ask the right question when it needed to be asked. We could also take a leaf out of his book and we could be much more honest in our relationships with others and with God. Thomas had the courage to ask. Like him we need not be afraid of doubts, questions and stuff we don't understand.

 Notes

Following Mum: Four ducklings follow their mother along the Rver Blackwater

JULY 4TH

'We are compelled to half-do a lot of things, to half-live our lives, half dream our dreams, half-love our loves. We have made ourselves into half people.' ~Brendan Kennelly

Am I a half person? Do I half live my life? It's an honest question that requires an honest answer. It is also a challenging question that could throw up a variety of answers. We know that for many people there is restlessness, a hunger for something more, an inner yearning that is not satisfied by what's on offer at the moment. If we are living half lives then we are always going to leave ourselves well short. In our Gospels Jesus said he came to bring life and that we could have it to the full. He was never into half measures but equally he never forced his offer on anyone. This hasn't changed today or never will. What has changed is the world we live in. The pace of change and momentum is relentless leaving us no option but to choose at times half lives. The invitation is to move some little bit beyond half. Even a fraction beyond half will be great progress.

 Notes

Cliff Views: The views along the cliffs of Moher in Co.Clare are always spectacular

JULY 5TH

'The voyage of my life at last has reached across a stormy sea, in a fragile boat. Neither painting nor sculpture will be able to calm my soul any longer.' –Michelangelo

Michelangelo is probably the most famous artist in the world. Millions have admired his work in the Sistine Chapel. He was an absolute genius with his work. Yet not as many know about his personal struggles in life. He also was a poet and it is through his writings that we get glimpses of his personal life. He died just short of his 90th birthday and in his final years he described his life as a fragile boat crossing a stormy sea. He questioned his faith and his beliefs. He felt unworthy and even rejected his own artwork. In his personal struggles he turned to God for help. All his life he tried to communicate the deepest mysteries of our faith in stone and paint. Here at the end was a man truggling. From his final works and writings we know he did find peace, comfort and healing. Whatever our age, we also are invited to turn to God with openness and honesty.

 Notes

Colourful Stairway: The flowers of the foxglove looking their best

JULY 6TH

'It's strange, significant, the way things come together – eventually even gentle curves create a circle.' ~Mary Murphy

The spiritual life is best described as a collection of gentle curves. Every curve of life in some way touches God. This means that God is connected to everything that happens throughout our lives. Even in difficult times we are helped and supported. Without such support we hit sharp corners. They are always difficult to negotiate straight-on. When it comes to spirituality we can choose the option of corners or curves. If we choose the option of curves or choose a sense of God in our lives, then those corners become much less of a hindrance. The invitation is to keep everything small and simple. Very few can work with complete circles. But all gentle curves do create a circle with time. God is incredibly patient and gentle with us. It is only ourselves and others who put expectations on us. There is an expectation to be a complete and perfect circle. It is an unfair expectation. Stick with small gentle curves and we're definitely on the right road.

 Notes

Ready For Picking: Gooseberries are ready for jam-making

JULY 7TH

'Prayer may not change things for you, but it sure changes you for things.' ~Samuel Shoemaker

Deep down we know the value of prayer. We know it's such an important link with God. We don't always get it right and maybe sometimes God doesn't always get it right either. The following little story will explain better. A little girl, dressed in her Sunday best, was running as fast as she could, trying not to be late for Sunday school. As she ran she prayed, "Dear Lord, please don't let me be late! Dear Lord, please don't let me be late!" While she was running and praying, she tripped on a kerb and fell, getting her clothes dirty and tearing her dress. She got up, brushed herself off, and started running again. As she ran she once again began to pray: "Dear Lord, please don't let me be late, but please don't shove me either!"

 Notes

Waterfall Views: A dog sits beside a waterfall at Coomatrush

JULY 8TH

'Heaven is not there up in the clouds. It is all around us.' ~Augustine Hoey

Belinda Carlisle had a hit in the 80s called, "Heaven Is A Place On Earth". She didn't quite say where but Heaven is closer than we think. It is something we all have different opinions on, without any one official account on what sort of a place it is. But that should not take from its significance. For believers the thought of Heaven is our ultimate goal and destination. It is a unique non-repeatable step on our journey towards completion and experiencing fullness of life. Are such thoughts a mere escape from the harsh realities of life? Not at all. It actually puts us more in touch with the rhythms of life. We know deep down that there must be something more, otherwise life is a boring cul-de-sac. Everything Jesus did in our Gospel stories was about bringing life and inviting people to new beginnings. He walked down many cul-de-sacs and pointed the way out of them. For Jesus, life is a constant repetition of new beginnings. Such a vision is encouraging and full of hope. It is also extended to us too.

 Notes

My Resting Place: A Dragonfly takes time out on a flower at Altamount, Millstreet

JULY 9TH

A story…

A well known Christian speaker was speaking to a large gathering and held up a €100 note. Then he asked who would like it and of course all hands went up. Then he said: "I will give this to you but first let me do this." With that he crushed the note, dropped it to the ground, stamped it with his shoe and picked it up, dirty and tattered. "Now who wants it?" he asked. Still the hands went into the air. He paused, put his hand up for silence and said: "My friends you have all learned a valuable lesson. No matter what I did to the money, you still wanted it because it did not decrease in value. Many times in our lives, we are crushed and ground into the dirt by the decisions we make and the circumstances that come our way. We feel as though we are worthless. But no matter what has happened or what will happen, not one of us will ever lose his or her value in God's eyes. To God, whether dirty or clean, crumpled or finely creased, we are still God's children and loved to bits. We are indeed priceless.

 Notes

Gigantic Spud: A big potato fills an entire dinner plate at Tooreenbawn

JULY 10TH

A summer blessing

May the beauty of God always surprise you.
May the freedom of God keep you centred and whole.
May the truthfulness of God bring peace to your heart.
May God's gift of Christ saturate you with love.
May the wisdom of God's dream always invite you deeper.
May the blessing of God in the company of Christ and the life-giving Spirit
guide you now and every minute of your life.
May you be open to God's gentle presence in your life this summer and
know that you are loved, cared for and always marked out as special.

 Notes

Ya Savage Boy!!: A bit of local slang suits this hungry seagull as he gulps down a fish in seconds

JULY 11TH

'Efficiency is doing better what is already being done.' ~Peter Drucker

An old lady went into a pharmacy and bought a packet of mothballs. The next day she returned and bought another packet. On the third day she did the same. When she appeared on the fourth day, the chemist could not restrain his curiosity. "You must have a lot of moths, Mrs Murphy?", he queried. "Yes I have" she replied. "And I've been throwing these balls at them for three days now and I haven't hit one yet!" We sometimes waste a lot of time, energy and effort in doing things each day that are simply not worth the effort. Often it is habit that keeps the momentum going. Even when it comes to spiritual matters we also waste a lot of time and energy. It's not always about long prayers, lots of words and aimless piety. Much more important is an honest relationship with God, some short but honest words from the heart and just to be open to what this day may bring. In what areas of my life could I be more efficient?

 Notes

How Old Are Ya!: Kieran McCarthy checks the age of a horse at Cahermee Fair in Buttevant

JULY 12TH

'Loneliness is about feeling that no one loves you and that no one cares. We can be lonely in a crowd, lonely in a family, lonely in a marriage or lonely in a church community. And yet how little it takes, to cure the desolation of loneliness.' ~Deborah Jones

Anyone can feel lonely. Most of us do from time to time. But for some, loneliness taints the whole of their life. Some turn to various forms of addictions to escape the loneliness. The most obvious one is alcohol, which can only bring us deeper into loneliness. There has to be something positive in everything, including loneliness. When we're lonely we can journey within. When we listen to our own loneliness we are really put in touch with ourselves. Maybe we don't always like what we see, but at least we're being honest. We help one another on that journey. Often it's the small things that make such a difference; a kind word, a smile, a text, a letter, a phone call or an invitation over for a cuppa. Who have I not made contact with a while? Could I make contact with them today or during the week?

 Notes

Rolling Hills: Some cows lie out in lovely sunshine on the lower slopes of Clara Mountain

JULY 13TH

'Fear imprisons while faith liberates. Fear paralyzes while faith empowers. Fear disheartens while faith encourages. Fear sickens while faith heals. Fear makes useless while faith makes serviceable. And most of all fear puts hopelessness at the heart of all while faith rejoices in God.' ~Harry Emerson Fosdick

Fear is something that is part and parcel of life. If we hadn't fear, we would have no sense of danger. But like all things there are limits and boundaries. Sometimes we allow fear to dominate and take over our lives. When this happens it imprisons, paralyzes, disheartens and puts us down. One of the best examples in our Gospels is the storm at sea and the disciples are frantic, fearful and angry with Jesus for his lack of concern at their plight. The response of Jesus was: "Why are you so afraid, have you no faith?" The invitation is to turn our fears over to God and allow God to calm, encourage and give us all a sense of hope.

 Notes

Working With Nature: Ger McSweeney checks the progress of a colony of bees

JULY 14TH

A story...

One day, a man found a cocoon of a butterfly. It had a small opening. He sat and watched the butterfly struggling to force its body through that little hole. Then it seemed to stop making any progress. The man decided to help the butterfly, took a pair of scissors, snipped off the remaining bit of the cocoon and the butterfly then emerged easily. But it had a swollen body and small, shriveled wings. The butterfly spent the rest of its life crawling around with a swollen body and shriveled wings. It never was able to fly. What the man, in his kindness and haste, did not understand was that the restricting cocoon and the struggle required for the butterfly to get through the tiny opening was nature's way of forcing fluid from the body of the butterfly into its wings so that it would be ready for flight once it achieved its freedom from the cocoon. Sometimes struggles are what we need in our lives. If we were allowed to go through life without any obstacles we would be weak, inexperienced, insensitive and out of touch with real life. Whatever our struggles we ask God for patience and the strength to get us through.

🖋 Notes

No Rain Please!!: Jodi Cronin and her bridesmaids are all smiles despite the rain at Blarney

JULY 15TH

'St.Swithin's Day, if it does rain, for forty days it will remain. St.Swithin's Day, if it be fair, for forty days it will rain no more' ~Old saying attributed to St.Swithin

Today is St.Swithin's Day. This is the most famous of all the weather related saints' days. St.Swithin died in 862AD and was buried outside Winchester Cathedral. Later when he was canonised a saint his body was instructed to be moved into a tomb within the cathedral. Legend has it that on the day the body was to be moved a storm broke on July 15th 971. It broke the end of a long dry spell and it continued to rain for a further 40 days after. This led the monks believing it was 'Divine Displeasure' and left the body in its original place. It is quite clear from weather records that there is little evidence to suggest 40 dry or 40 wet days following a dry or wet St.Swithin's Day. But one thing we do know with certainty is that good weather is vitally important to the farming community and holiday makers at this time of year. We pray that good, dry, fine and sunny weather will prevail for the coming weeks.

 Notes

Nearly Ripe: A field of barley is making great progress

JULY 16TH

'This is the day the Lord has made, let us rejoice and be glad in it.' ~Psalm 118:24

A good day doesn't just happen. It requires first of all from us commitment, openness and good intention. If we sit back and hope that today will be good then we will surely be disappointed. There is a world of experience and wisdom to suggest that we can have a strong influence on what happens in any given day. No matter what comes our way we have a choice in how we respond. We can be fearful, pessimistic and dismissive or we can be positive, courageous and hopeful. Why bother trying to be positive and upbeat when there is so much negativity around? Negativity tends to attract all sorts of other negativity around us. That's why the Christian message is upbeat and positive. In the middle of darkness and negativity we need light, hope and a sense of positive. Today may be very ordinary, it is far from perfect but it's the only day we can really work with and make the most of.

 Notes

Splash Of Yellow: These flowers add plenty of summer colour

JULY 17TH

'The purest and most thoughtful minds are those which love colour the most.' ~*John Ruskin*

We are all affected by colours that we see around us each day.
The colour of our clothes often picks up our mood and how we are feeling.
Nature provides many contrasts of colours. Different flowers planted in different ways can give many variations of colour. During these weeks of July our gardens are full of summer colour. The same goes for us in relation to colours as well. On our own we're just one colour, but working together as God's family can bring the best of colours together. We're good at seeing the colour and positives of others but much slower in believing what we have. The message of the Gospels is quite clear. Be proud of who you are, be proud of your colours and share as many of them as you can with others.

 Notes

Maturing: These three cygnets are maturing nicely at Altamount Gardens, near Tullow, Co.Carlow

JULY 18TH

A little humour......

A woman had been driving for many hours and she decided to take a rest. She drove on to a side road, turned off the car engine, closed her eyes and fell into a deep sleep. A man out jogging knocked on her window, scaring her. "Sorry to wake you but can you tell me what time it is?" The woman glanced at her watch. "7.15" she said through the glass. "Thank you" the jogger said and left. "Just my luck", the woman muttered angrily, "I'm parked on someone's jogging route." Then she tried to get back to sleep when there was a knock on the window. It was another jogger! "Do you have the time?" The woman sighed, "It's 7.20" "Thanks" said the jogger and trotted off. She looked down the road and saw more joggers coming her way. Irritated, she wrote down on a large sheet "I DON'T KNOW THE TIME" and put it on the window and settled back to sleep. Just as she was dozing off a jogger knocked on the window. The woman pointed to the sign and shouted, "Can't you read?" "I sure can ma'am. I just wanted to let you know. It's 7.30"

 Notes

Galloping Views: The view looking across to Courtmacsherry through the feet of galloping horses at the annual Courtmacsherry races

JULY 19TH

The most famous book in the world is of course the Bible. It has inspired millions and given so many renewed direction and hope. If one could summarise it in a few lines the following reflection is a good attempt.

Miracles do happen. Somebody loves me, constantly and consistently. I am not alone. Love transforms people. The majority are not always right. Wonderful things can happen in the darkest moments of our lives because of the Resurrection. Things can often look better in three days. Death is a transition not an end in itself. All things can work together for good. A sigh can become a song. Tomorrow does not have to be the same as today or yesterday. There is a light behind every shadow. We get what we give and equally we find what we expect. One person can make a difference especially the person of Jesus in our lives.

 Notes

Land Of The Midnight Sun: During the summer months the sunsets in Norway are simply breath-taking. The sky fills with breathtaking colour and it can hold this for hours evolving into deeper and more spectacular colour

JULY 20TH

'We are complex people carrying our own wounds that make us determined to go it alone, to nurse our hurts and regrets and to maintain our pride at all costs.' ~Gary Wade

We will always be uniquely complex individuals. Mystery makes up life and is part of every single person. There will always be a part of us that others will never understand. Equally we can never fully understand everything about someone else. While it is true that others may not fully understand our hurt, pain, confusion, isolation, anger or whatever is going on for us, we should never have to go it alone. No person can journey through life carrying it all on their own. That is why there is always such relief when we can just share and talk about what's going on for us. In sharing it, there is a great release from the pressure of going it alone. If you follow the life story of Jesus in our Gospels, it was all about how he allowed other people share their story. There was no room for solo runs or isolation but all about including every person's story, no matter how dark or painful.

 Notes

Sliding Along: A caterpillar slides along a rhubarb leaf to its next food source

JULY 21ST

'Every one of us is permeated with the presence of God. The Pope does not have it any more than the truck driver or the nurse. Within our own hearts is this same God bursting to life in us.' ~*Michael Morwood*

God is closer to each of us than we can possibly ever imagine. If we look into our own hearts or into our own lives we will find God. It seems we are content to look for God elsewhere and end up disappointed. Many still see God as one who rewards and punishes. When things go wrong in life the explanation is that God must be testing or punishing them. Some refer to it as carrying a cross or that it must be God's will if some tragedy occurs. Such viewpoints are deeply ingrained in our traditions and are not helpful. What sort of a God gets a kick out of misfortune? Jesus in our Gospels makes it quite clear that God does not punish. God is very much in the here and now, God loves us no matter what's going on for us, and God is not to be feared.

 Notes

Happy Family: A family of Alpacas with their young, called cria, taken on the farm of the Casey family

JULY 22ND

The following reflection is called 'What I've Learned'. The author is unknown and part two comes tomorrow.

I've learned that you cannot make someone love you. All you can do is be someone who can be loved. The rest is up to them. I've learned that no matter how much I care, some people just don't care back. I've learned that it takes years to build up trust and only seconds to destroy it. I've learned that it's not what you have in your life but who you have in your life that counts. I've learned that you shouldn't compare yourself to the best others can do. I've learned that you can do something in an instant that will give you heartache for life. I've learned that it's taking me a long time to become the person I want to be. I've learned that you should always leave loved ones with loving words. It may be the last time you see them. I've learned that you can keep going long after you think you can't. I've learned that we are responsible for what we do, no matter how we feel. I've learned that heroes are the people who do what has to be done, when it needs to be done.

 Notes

Summer Raindrops: A basket of pansies becomes a raindrop collector

JULY 23RD

The following is another piece from the reflection called 'What I've Learned'.

I've learned that two people can look at exactly the same thing and see something totally different. I've learned that sometimes the people you expect to kick you when you're down will be the ones to help you get back up again. I've learned that just because someone doesn't love the way you want them to, doesn't mean they don't love you with all they have. I've learned that maturity has more to do with the types of experiences you've had and what you've learned from them and less to do with how many birthdays you've celebrated. I've learned that no matter how good a friend is, they're going to hurt you every once in a while and you must forgive them for that. I've learned that it isn't always enough to be forgiven by others. Sometimes you have to learn to forgive yourself. I've learned that our background and circumstances may have influenced who we are, but we are responsible for who we become.

 Notes

Making My Way Up: A six spotted Burmese moth makes its way up a flower

JULY 24TH

'A society without God is a society without a compass.' ~Pope Benedict XVI

With huge advances in technology and the arrival of satellite navigation systems, it might seem that a compass is a thing of the past. But it still plays a very important role in land and sea navigation. There are many ways to describe the importance of something but comparing God to a compass is simple but clever. Life at the best of times is complex, fragile, with unexpected twists and turns each day. No person can be prepared for every eventuality but we can have the basics ready to help us cope and adapt. If God is present in our lives we are at a distinct advantage. We are in a better position to cope, to find our feet, to adapt, to get renewed strength and to start again on our journey.

 Notes

Rare Beauty: An Amur Tiger looks happy and content in summer sunshine at Dublin Zoo

JULY 25TH

'We are only the earthenware jars that hold this treasure, to make it clear that such an overwhelming power comes from God and not from us.' ~2 Corinthians 4:7

The image of an earthenware jar is simple and yet so powerful when we look at it closer. An earthenware jar is fragile and is made of baked clay. It is symbolic of all that's fragile, particularly in our world and in our lives. Yet we are told it holds a great treasure despite its fragility and ours. It also reflects our own lives. We are indeed fragile and vulnerable. Despite our best efforts we have little control over what is fragile and unpredictable in life. Yet we give the impression at times that we are unbreakable, important and beyond any limitation. No person can be fully any of these. Like an earthenware jar, we are limited and finite. We can't journey through life thinking we're invincible. The real treasure is an ability to invite God into the fragility of our lives, whatever it might be right now.

 Notes

Hurley Tunnel: Deirdre Coughlan and Cathal McCarthy at the Church of St.Michael, Rathbarry, west Cork

JULY 26TH

'Enterprising doesn't just relate to the ability to make money. Being enterprising also means feeling good enough about yourself, having enough self-worth to want to seek advantages and opportunities that will make a difference to your future.' ~Jim Rohn

Money may make the world go round but there are many things in life that no amount of money can buy. Many today seem to have a low sense of self worth or don't feel confident enough in their own unique abilities. This is a great pity. At the heart of all our Gospel stories is about Jesus wanting to instil confidence and belief into everyone he met. Many of the stories recall how people were transformed, bubbling over with a sense of freedom and new beginnings. Such a feel-good factor wasn't false or temporary. It was life-changing. Do I trust and believe in my own abilities? Can I take one positive step forward today? Can I help someone I know feel better about themselves?

 Notes

Mr.Scarecrow!: A scarecrow keeps the crows at bay in a field of barley

JULY 27TH

'Suffering is something that we all understand and love is the language that heals all suffering. All of us have this gift to give to others through our eyes, our embrace and our words, through shared tears or a kind deed or prayer.' ~Ronan Scully

Suffering is something we are all very much aware of. It affects us all in different ways. It is something that none of us can avoid. But it is often misunderstood. Some see suffering as a test or a punishment from God. This is never the case. Suffering is one of the many complexities that make up the mystery of life. At the heart of our belief system is a God who helps us through the many complexities of life. God is love and love is the greatest healer of them all when we face suffering of any kind.

 Notes

Weighed Down: A poppy flower is weighed down during heavy rainfall

JULY 28TH

A man came into the doctor's surgery one day and he was very worried. He explained his problem, "Every part of my body that I touch is very sore, my nose, my elbow, my head, my left hand." The doctor gave him a thorough examination, x-ray, blood tests etc. The man returned the next day for the results and was very nervous. "Did you find out what's wrong with me?" he asked the doctor. "I did" he replied. "What is it?" enquired the very worried patient. "All that's wrong with you" replied the doctor, "is that your finger is broken!"

We often think the worst. We worry and fret about many things. Many of them are outside our control. Even if they were within our control we'd still be nervous and anxious. In our Gospels, Jesus called for a change of mindset. Instead of a closed, negative outlook, he called on people to think positive, to trust in God and to know that everything is not as bad is it first seems.

 Notes

Please Stop!: Peter Wills makes sure the train is going to stop at Millstreet Railway Station

JULY 29TH

'We must cut our coat according to our cloth and adapt ourselves to changing circumstances.' ~W.R. Inge

Most homes have a thermometer and a thermostat. What is the difference between the two? A thermometer merely tells what the temperature is in a particular room. If you move it from a cold room to a warm room, it will rise and change to register what that temperature may be. It always adjusts to its environment. The thermostat is different because it adjusts the room temperature. If you want a fixed temperature to save on high energy bills the thermostat is your friend. It will regulate the heating at whatever temperature you want. In life we are either a thermostat or a thermometer. We can either blend in with the crowd (thermometer) or we can make a difference (thermostat). In our Gospels Jesus calls us to become thermostats. Instead of going with everything and anything we are instead called to be people with conviction, self belief, a sense of pride and that we have something genuine to offer. Like a thermostat we can and do make a difference. Unlike a thermometer that can be all over the place and unsure of where to go next, we can like a thermostat find a balance in our lives that's good, healthy and important. Are you a thermometer or a thermostat?

Notes

Simply Delicious: A bowl of strawberries is very inviting at La Cala de Mijas in Spain

JULY 30TH

'It is never too late to be what you might have been' ~George Eliot

One constant theme throughout the scriptures is how God never closes the door on anyone. Even when people tested, ignored and abandoned God, the door was never closed. The very same happens today. God gently reminds us that it is never too late to be what we were created for. All of us no doubt have things we want to do and we have hopes for the future. Just because things haven't worked out for us back along should not be a reason to throw the towel in. It is never too late to make a fresh start, to retry and to be open to new beginnings. Others may close the door on us but at least with God the door is always open. Have I thrown the towel in? Do I feel it's too late to restart? Can I begin to trust myself and begin to do something I have been putting off for a long time?

 Notes

Waterslide: A fine summers day ensures plenty of fun at the weir in Ballincollig Regional Park

JULY 31ST

'Deep within us, there is a spirit of judgement and we are often harshest on ourselves. Because a part of us may be disordered, we condemn the whole of ourselves. Somehow we are attracted to the darkness rather than the light.' ~Martin Tierney

We are indeed our own worst enemies. We can be so cruel on ourselves. We judge ourselves critically, we condemn ourselves and we so often put ourselves down. If it was put along-side all our good and strong points, there would simply be no contest. We all know in sport how some teams who seem completely lost and out of a match can turn it round. Often it's the half-time team talk that can spark life and a sense of purpose. It reflects on us too. Why should negativity, some mistake or weakness on our part overshadow everything else? Can I simply be less harsh on myself and much more kind?

 Notes

AUGUST

Fishy Feeling: Lorna Doherty from Coláiste Choilm has a fishy feeling at the English Market, Cork

AUGUST 1ST

'Being created anew is a desire of many of us. We want to start fresh, do it better, transform our lives and live more deeply. But we get stuck and lose our way. We yearn for more meaningful lives but we get co-opted by the superficial values of our society.' ~Edward L.Beck

A new and fresh start can be liberating. It can open up a whole new set of horizons for us. But our initial enthusiasm is not always followed through by a consistent plan. We tend to stumble and lose our way. It's like the effects of a big magnet and we get pulled back into our old ways and old habits. We then lose confidence and eventually give up. It is even truer of all things spiritual. How many times have we made an effort to prioritise our spiritual lives, only to find our best plans pushed aside by busyness and other priorities? Making a fresh start is something we should not give up on. Perhaps more manageable and realistic goals is the way to go. Any new path requires effort, commitment and enthusiasm. We pray to God today to help us make it happen.

 Notes

Meadow Colour: These flowers provide a purple carpet through a meadow at Avoca, Co.Wicklow

AUGUST 2ND

What is a typical day in the life of a priest? Every day is different, but the following on display in Galway Cathedral will give some clues:

My husband has left me – Can you spare a fiver? I'm out on the streets – Bless me Father for I have sinned – Can you bless our house? – Will you say a prayer that I'll get the interview? – Sarah's living with her boyfriend – Come up later for the tea – Eddie has given up his faith – What made you become a priest? – The organist refuses to play that! – Alex wants to be Confirmed – The folk group has walked out – Dad's been sent to prison – Deirdre's on drugs – Father come quickly our mother is dying – Owen doesn't want to serve Mass any more – Can I marry a Buddhist in a Church ceremony? – My girlfriend is having an abortion – Will you teach me how to pray? – Can you say Mass with the youth group next week? – We want to get married – I'd say she could do with a chat – Do you do Baptisms on a Friday? – The Bishop wants your help with something, will you call to his house this evening – Something's really bothering me Father and I've never told this to anyone before.

 Notes

Morning Call: A Guinea fowl makes its voice heard at dawn on Cape Clear Island, west Cork

AUGUST 3RD

A reflection called 'The World Goes On'...

If we pause for a moment and briefly forget all that we have to do. If we can pause for those few moments and if we can forget everything, we will make a surprising discovery. We will discover that the world actually goes on without us. This means that all we do and all our rushing about is not as important as we imagine. If we can realise this that the world will actually go on without us a healing process begins. We begin to relax in the presence of God. We begin to realise that everything around us is pure gift to be enjoyed and appreciated. We begin to understand that the most important thing is just being ourselves. We surrender ourselves into God's hands, taking it one day at a time. We are at peace knowing that hectic, shallow and frenzied activity serves no real purpose. What can I do or where can I go to help me appreciate that today is pure gift to be enjoyed and appreciated?

 Notes

Mum You Know I Love You!: A private moment with a pig and her piglet at Muckross Traditional Farm, Killarney

AUGUST 4TH

The following reflection is called 'For A Reason'. The author is unknown.

Sometimes people come into your life and you know right away that they were meant to be there. They serve some sort of purpose, teach you a lesson or help figure out who you are or who you want to become. Everything happens for a reason. Nothing happens by chance or by means of good or bad luck. Without the small tests we go through each day, life would be like a smoothly paved, straight and flat road to nowhere. It would be safe and comfortable but dull and utterly pointless. If someone hurts you, betrays or breaks your heart, forgive them, for they have helped you learn about trust and the importance of being cautious to who you open your heart to. Hold your head up because you have every right to. Tell yourself you are a great individual and believe in yourself, for if you don't believe in yourself, no-one else will believe in you either. You can make of your life anything you wish. Create your own life and then go out and live it.

 Notes

Going, Going Gone!: Jennifer Murphy enjoying a lighter moment at Shanagarry, Co.Cork

AUGUST 5TH

It's All In What You Say…

"I got 2 As in my exam", the small boy shouted. His voice was filled with glee. But his father very bluntly asked, "Why did you not get three?" "Mum I've got the dishes done", the girl called from the door. But her mother very calmly said, "And did you sweep the floor?" "I've mowed the grass", the tall boy said, "and I've put the mower away". But his father asked him with a shrug, "Did you clean the lawnmower after you?" The children in the house next door seem happy and content. The same things happened over there. But this is how it went. "I got 2 As in my exam", the small boy shouted. His voice was filled with glee. His father proudly said "That's great you really have made my day." "Mum I've got the dishes done", the girl called from the door. Her mother smiled and said, "Thank you so much, I really appreciate what you have done." "I've mowed the grass", the tall boy said, "and I've put the mower away". His father answered, "That's great and you did a great job too."

 Notes

My Masterpiece: A spider waiting for for his dinner

AUGUST 6TH

'Now I am revealing new things to you, things hidden and unknown to you, created just now. This very moment you have heard nothing of these things until now, so that you cannot say, 'Oh yes, I knew all this'. ~Isaiah 48:6

We sometimes think of God, religion and spirituality as just static. Some see it as created in the past which has been passed onto us to preserve and in turn we pass it on to someone else. This is very limiting. Everything about God is fresh, moving and changing. Nothing stays still. We can never say we know God fully or that we know what God's plans are for us. Each day we can learn something new about ourselves, about God, about life, about the world we live in, about our family, our friends and so on. All of them are never in isolation but are connected in a mysterious web that make up today. God is never boring, dull or static. If we believe that today is God's gift to us then we are open to possibility, freshness and a sense of freedom in our lives. The invitation is to be open to God's many blessings that make up each day.

 Notes

Harvest Time: Some crab apples turning a lovely red colour

AUGUST 7TH

'We need to ensure that we never let despair or hopelessness or despondency overwhelm us. We need to know that as human beings created by God with all our imperfections and our talents, that there is another way. We know that we shall overcome.' ~Bryan Dobson

As a human race we are tough and resilient. Yes we are vulnerable, weak and frail at times but deep down there is an inbuilt strength within each person to keep going. During tough times we rely on this inbuilt strength even more. Some call it hope, some call it being optimistic and some call it faith. But no matter how bad things may be, there is another way. There is always a solution to a crisis, always light after darkness, always calm after a storm, always possibilities in bleakness and always a God to gently guide us through to where we need to go. This is the other way. It is easy to lose sight of this way but we must keep it in sight at all times.

 Notes

Massive Jump: Neal Fearon on 'Candileto 4' jumps the Land Rover Puissance wall at 7' 4" at the RDS, Dublin

AUGUST 8TH

'We're all familiar with the expression "straddling the fence". We criticise people for doing it and we do it ourselves sometimes too. Straddling the fence is about refusing to make a clear decision about something.' ~Joseph Slattery

It's fair to say that many of us are experts at straddling the fence. We want the best of both worlds. It also happens in our relationship with God and our everyday lives. We want to believe that we are in with God and we also want to believe that we are in touch with all that is happening in our lives. What tends to happen is that we push anything spiritual into a box of its own and only open it when we want to or when we're in the mood. We sometimes don't connect God with our own lives. So instead of straddling the fence and trying to have a foot in both camps, why not take down the fence? Why not try and integrate our connection with God and what goes on in our everyday lives. So instead of pushing God into a box, why not allow God to be a part of all that's going in our lives. This is where real growth can take place.

 Notes

Seal Island: A colony of seals relax on an island out in Kenmare Bay, Co.Kerry

AUGUST 9TH

'Heaven's Grocery Store' ~Author Unknown

One day I was walking down one of life's many roads. Then I saw a sign that read 'Heaven's Grocery Store'. As I got a little closer a door opened and in I went. I met an angel who said, "My child, shop with care. Everything you need for life is in this store, carry all you want." First I got some patience. Love was in the same row. Further down was understanding. I made sure to pick that up as you need it all the time. I picked up wisdom and a bag or two of faith. I stopped to pick up some strength and courage. I made sure to pick up love too, it was everywhere. As I went up the aisle I saw prayer and I had to put that in too. Peace and joy were plentiful as were song, praise and thanksgiving. Then I asked the angel, "How much do I owe?" The angel said, "Take them everywhere you go." And then I said again, "But really how much do I owe you?" The angel smiled and said, "My child, Jesus paid your bill a long time ago."

 Notes

I'm Heading Straight For You! A young fox is out for an early morning stroll

AUGUST 10TH

'Ordinary riches can be stolen, real riches cannot. In your soul are infinitely precious things that cannot be taken from you.' ~Oscar Wilde

There are many things that can be taken from us in life. Even under lock and key, nothing is absolutely safe. But there are many things within each of us that are just so precious. These are special and unique to you. They are in that sacred place called the soul of each person. Your faith may be barely hanging in there, lukewarm or deep rooted. But it can never take from what's special to you. The problem is that so many completely ignore the vast treasures within each of us. Our world may not be the nicest of places at times, but there is such a reserve of deep love in so many people that it can't be ignored. This deep reserve is God's most precious gift to each of us.

 Notes

Double Clear!!: These two dogs show how its done at Tullamore Show, Co.Offaly

AUGUST 11TH

The following prayer was written by Marjorie Ahern:

I have the power to choose to see things as they really are. I choose to see things as God does, with the eyes of love. Since it is the nature of God to be present everywhere, I know that all there really is in this entire universe is the love of God. The love of God surrounds me, dwells within me, goes before me and soothes the way for me. I am a beloved child of the universe and the universe lovingly takes care of me now and forevermore. When I need something, I turn to God who created me. I ask for what I need and then I give thanks even before receiving, knowing that it will come to me in the perfect time, space and sequence. Amen

 Notes

Clinging On: A bumble bee holds on tight as it gathers nectar from a Fuchia flower

AUGUST 12TH

'Those who speak most of progress measure it by quantity and not by quality' ~George Santayana

Progress in our modern world has been hectic and frantic. The pace of change can be described as wonderful or frightening. There is no denying that we have made great progress in terms of technology, quality of living and more opportunities. But have we sacrificed quality for quantity? Have we let go of important values? Do we prioritise time for each other, time to listen, time to nourish what's important and time to be there for each other. Or are we too busy caught up in the world of quantity instead of quality. God always encourages us to make quality time and especially to prioritise those quiet down-to-earth ordinary moments where God is often present. God isn't into deadlines, quotas or time constraints. I don't have to be a slave to quantity and trying to get everything done. Today and during the week I can prioritise quality time.

 Notes

Explosion Of Colour: A thistle flower bursts into colour

AUGUST 13TH

'A fool always finds a greater fool to admire them.' ~Author Unknown

We've all done foolish things with no exception. At the time it was not what we planned and it may even have initially seemed right at the time, but the end result was that we made a fool of ourselves. But we really become a fool when we begin to wallow in self pity and when we think the whole world is watching, laughing and enjoying what we've done wrong. It's time to move on. It's time to leave it behind and make some sort of a fresh start today. The Gospels bubble with freshness and new beginnings. With Jesus no-ones story was so bad or foolish to upset him. He simply said: "You are forgiven, move on and make a fresh start in your life." Can I leave something foolish I have done behind me and move on with my life?

 Notes

Waiting Patiently: A dog waits patiently for its master to come home

AUGUST 14TH

'Our huffing and puffing to impress God, our frantic scramble for brownie points and our wallowing in guilt are a flat denial of the gospel of grace.' ~Martin Tierney

What is grace? It's a question that would send many heads turning if it was asked at a table quiz! It has nothing to do with Grace Before Meals! Grace could best be described as God showering me with blessings and love. I may feel I don't deserve them, I may feel I have let God down, I may feel unworthy but if that's our thinking, we are wide of the mark. God always sees things in a different light. We seem to have a natural inclination to embrace negativity. But God always focuses in on goodness, love, creativity, life, energy, inclusiveness and so on. One could sum it up in one word - grace. Through the grace of God, today is a good day to be alive and a good day to make the most of what comes my way.

 Notes

Surrounded By Love: A stained glass window of Mary at Knock Shrine, Co.Mayo

AUGUST 15TH

'The Feast of the Assumption which we celebrate today is a day that marks time. The life of Mary has marked time for all humanity. She gave us the waiting time, the birthing time and the growing-up time. She gave us the letting-go time, the painful time, the dying time and the rising time. Today we watch her as she moves into eternal time.' ~*Michael Mullaney*

Today's feast day is a time of year when things are changing around us. Days are getting shorter, back to school is just around the corner and the hint of autumn is gently creeping in. Mary's feast gives us a little nudge to make the most of the remainder of this month. At a deeper level it gives us a nudge to appreciate what Mary means to us. Her asscension into Heaven might give the impression that she is aloof, irrelevant and out of touch. What it really means is that she is a truly great friend to have as we journey through life. She is closer to us than we can possibly imagine. She is especially close to our every experience. We ask for her guidance, direction and many blessings on each of us today.

 Notes

Jumping High: A kite surfer jumps high at Lahinch, Co.Clare

AUGUST 16TH

I realized that there were occasions when I needed to be able to learn to be alongside people without being able to do anything that would make them better or happier. There are times when presence is all you have to offer. ~Angela Tilby

One day a small boy was trying to lift a heavy stone, but he couldn't budge it. His father passing by stopped to watch his son's efforts. Finally he said to his son: "Are you using all your strength?" Exasperated, the boy cried, "Yes I am." "No you're not", said the father calmly, "You haven't asked me to help you." Sometimes we try and deal with problems and worries all by our self. It's not an easy thing to do and nearly always an impossible task. But with the help of someone it can become so manageable. So if there is something bothering or upsetting us, it might be good to share it with someone else. Like the father in the story we might be called to be there for someone and sometimes we need to take the initiative. Our presence can be the greatest gift to someone and its impact often goes way beyond what we might ever think.

 Notes

No Fear Of Heights: These two dogs admire the views at Carraroe, Co.Galway

AUGUST 17TH

Christian prayer is not an attempt to move out of mundane human life but rather to enter into it more fully. If prayer is not to be hypocritical, it must come from the heart, from the centre of our being, from the reality of our lives rather than from our lips. ~*Joseph Schmidt*

There are indeed many forms of prayer. There is one form of prayer that is unique to everyone and that is praying our daily experience or whatever is going on in our own lives. It calls for great honesty. Formal prayer may not always help us to get in touch with the totally unique and private happenings in our own lives. But if our own prayer is honest and in some way touches on all that's going on in our lives, then we are on to a winner. It allows us to be simply present to God in the unfolding story of our daily lives. Can I set aside some few minutes to reflect and pray on all that's happening in my life at the moment?

 Notes

Fruits Of The Summer: Raspberries waiting to be picked

AUGUST 18TH

The following story is food for thought:

In the faint light of the attic, an old man, tall and stooped, bent his great frame and made his way to a stack of boxes that sat near one of the little half-windows. Brushing aside a wisp of cobwebs, he tilted the top box toward the light and began to carefully lift out one old photograph album after another and his old journal. Opening the yellowed pages, he glanced over a short reading, and his lips curved in an unconscious smile. His eyes brightened as he read the words that spoke clear and sweet to his soul as he read the inscription for Aug 18th. It stood out because it was so brief in comparison to other days. In his own neat handwriting were these words: 'Wasted the whole day fishing with Jimmy. Didn't catch a thing.' With a deep sigh and a shaking hand, he took up Jimmy's journal and found the boy's entry for the same day. Large scrawling letters, pressed deeply into the paper, read: 'Went fishing with my dad. Best day of my life.'

 Notes

Fancy Hairdo: A peacock looking its best at Altamount House, Tullow, Co.Carlow

AUGUST 19TH

'Perhaps once in a hundred years a person may be ruined by excessive praise, but surely once every minute someone dies inside for lack of it.' ~Cecil Osborne

It's been said so many times how we're quick to find fault and so slow to give praise and encouragement. This is not a new phenomenon that has recently started. Even Jesus recognised how people were slow to encourage, give praise and show appreciation. A few words of praise may seem hardly worth the effort but to someone else they can mean so much. There are many people out there who are quietly struggling, finding it difficult and doing their best to keep going. A friendly word or a word of praise can give such a boost and lift. Is there anyone close and near to me who could do with a word of praise? Today is infinitely better than leaving it until tomorrow.

 Notes

Steep Climb: Riders in the Pro Tour Of Ireland climbing up Curragh Mountain near Millstreet with Lance Armstrong on the far right

AUGUST 20TH

'Love is the light and in the end the only light that can always illuminate a world grown dim. Love is possible and we are able to practice it because we are created in the image of God.' ~Pope Benedict XVI

Much has been written about love but sometimes the most carefully chosen words do not always do it justice. The words of Pope Benedict are so appropriate and uplifting. It gives great courage and hope to all of us, particularly those areas of our lives that have grown dim. We have all experienced its impact during times of doubt, tragedy and suffering. We often don't know what to say. Sometimes there are no words. But deep down we know that God's presence is felt at the very time when the only thing to do is love. A verse from a poem puts it so well: "Love never dies. So when all that's left is love, make sure you keep giving it away, today and every day."

 Notes

Determination: Amy Collins from Coláiste Choilm shows her commitment and determination in climbing a cliff face at Cappanalea Co.Kerry

AUGUST 21ST

'We are indeed much more than what we eat, but what we eat can nevertheless help us to be much more than what we are.' ~Adelle Davis

In the western world one third of all food purchased in households is thrown away. Much of this food discarded is actually in date and perfectly useable. In England alone we're told that 1.3 million cartons of yoghurt are thrown out each day. Such wastage of food can best be described as shocking and a sad reflection on all of us. It's not that we can point the finger of blame at others. We've all been there and we've all thrown food out carelessly. We live in abundance, whereas in many parts of the world it's survival on little and nothing. Do I throw out food? Do I buy and cook more than I need? Do I give in to so-called special offers in supermarkets and stuff I don't want? We thank God for the food we eat each day, food that is our lifeline, nourishing and wholesome. May we never waste it or take it for granted.

 Notes

Whizzing By: A karter at 70kph slides the kart through a corner at Watergrasshill karting track

AUGUST 22ND

'Be at peace with your own soul, then Heaven and Earth will be at peace with you.' ~St.Jerome

There is a story told about a young man who got involved with a tough gang. He desperately wanted to be one of them. He forced himself to be the hard man, to talk with a brash tongue and to act hostile towards people. This he felt was what was expected of him. Then one day he met a young woman who was wise beyond her years. She liked him and saw a side of him that he was trying to hide. She said: "Do you know that deep down you are a gentle person with a big, kind heart? Why are you so afraid that someone might see it?" It was what he needed to hear and became a turning point in his life. Our good and especially our best is often hidden away. Can I bring it out in someone else by simply telling them what it is? Such honesty can be life-giving and life-changing.

 Notes

Years Of Growth: A male British Alpine goat stands proud and tall on Cape Clear Island, west Cork

AUGUST 23RD

'Their poverty and level of fragile existence cripples them even from realizing the enormity of the injustice they have to endure. They are deprived of everything decent and human, even the right to be angry at the world, at government and at God. They endure all, they suffer all and they are silent about it.' ~Fr.Shay Cullen speaking on a visit to a huge rubbish dump in the Philippines where an estimated 80,000 live on or near the dump known as Payatas

Fr.Shay Cullen is well known for his work with the poorest of the poor. For many years he has been a brave and courageous voice speaking on behalf of those who have no one to speak for them. In this particular dump he talks about how locals wade ankle deep in the filth, struggling to live on human waste and decay. Small children work as hard as adults, scratching the trash with hooks and grabbing anything that might bring them a few coins and a mouthful of food. Working with the poorest of the poor has not deterred Fr.Shay or his fellow workers. Strange as it may seem, they talk about working on holy ground. Somehow in the dirt and smell God is present. When we complain, give out, sulk and make a big commotion about little things, we might well remember those who live and work in the Payatas.

 Notes

Purple Forest: These colourful flowers stand tall and upright

AUGUST 24TH

How rich are the depths of God - how deep is God's wisdom and knowledge and how impossible to
penetrate God's motives or understand God's methods. Who could ever know the mind of the Lord?
~St Paul's letter to the Romans 11:33-34

These lines are one of the most beautiful that Paul wrote. These lines were not just written for the sake of putting a few lines together. They were written by Paul over much reflection on how he felt God was present in his life. Like all of us Paul grappled with the great issues of life only to end up in admiration of God's boundless wisdom. Paul had a great appreciation of the richness and depths of God's blessings in his life. Sometimes we might not be as confident or as sure as Paul. But with careful reflection we know that we can point to God's influence and presence in our lives. Such an influence and presence has been a cornerstone of our lives. No event or person can ever take it away from us.

 Notes

Rose Of Tralee: The Rose Of Tralee festival reminding us that back-to-school is upon us!

AUGUST 25TH

'Every great player has learned the two Cs: how to concentrate and how to maintain composure.'
~Byron Nelson

There is a story told about St.Francis of Sales. He observed the custom of the country area where he was living. He noticed a farm servant going across a farmyard to draw water at the well. Before she lifted the bucket, the girl always put a piece of wood into it. One day Francis asked the girl, "Why do you do that?" She looked surprised and answered, as if it were a matter of course, "It's to keep the water from spilling. By concentrating on the piece of wood I can keep the water steady." Life can be such a mixture of different things happening. Sometimes we can be all over the place and sometimes it's good to have something to help us concentrate. Our piece of wood could be a simple prayer. It can help us keep life in perspective.

 Notes

Midnight Mirror Reflections: A boat stands perfectly still at midnight just off Flatanger, north west Norway

AUGUST 26TH

The following prayer for strength was written by Pope John 23rd

Every day, I need you Lord, but today especially I need some extra strength to face whatever is to come. This day, more than any other day, I need to feel you near me to strengthen my courage and to overcome my fear. By myself I cannot meet the challenge of the hour. We are frail human creatures and we need a Higher Power to sustain us in all that life may bring. And so dear Lord, hold my trembling hand. Be with me Lord this day and stretch out your powerful arm to help me. May your love be upon me as I place all my hope in you. Amen.

 Notes

Torpedo!: A heron flying through at top speed over the River Blackwater

AUGUST 27TH

'The stone which the builders rejected as worthless turned out to be the most important of all.'
~Mark 12:10

In years gone by horse-shoe nails were common and important. Today, horses have no input in our public transport system. It was so different years ago and horse-shoe nails could often be found at the side of the road. Benjamin Franklin in one of his poems wrote: "For want of a nail the shoe was lost. For want of a shoe the horse was lost. For want of a horse the rider was lost. For want of a rider the battle was lost." One nail here made all the difference. So often it's the humble one that can make all the difference. It could be a simple smile, a word of thanks, a little gift, a text, a phone call, a hug, a get-well wish, a prayer and so on. On its own it may look insignificant, but it often will turn out to be the most important of all.

 Notes

Girl Power: These ladies putting their best foot forward as organisers of the Ballinlough Community Family Day

AUGUST 28TH

'One of the rights I treasure most greatly in my life is my right to be wrong. I absolutely demand this right. I demand the right to be wrong one hundred times a day, in big things and small things. I could surrender many other rights and still live a satisfying life but I could not survive a single day without the right to be wrong.' ~Geoffrey Robinson

An ability to be able to say 'I'm sorry' can be powerful. I'm sure we can recall moments in our own lives when we didn't do so and we know we should have. Perhaps there was an element of pride or a fear of feeling vulnerable and weak to say sorry. No matter what our age, to say we got it wrong isn't the end of the world. It implies honesty and openness. It implies that we are willing to move on and try again. It doesn't mean that we will never get it wrong again, but it does mean we are willing to give it our best. Our ability to say sorry may be rusty. Is there anyone in my life who I need to say sorry to?

 Notes

Sweet Berry: A hungry wasp finds food in this clump of blackberries

AUGUST 29TH

From Parent to Teenager…

I gave you life but I cannot live it for you. I can teach you things but I cannot make you learn. I can allow you freedom but I cannot account for you. I can take you to church but I cannot make you believe. I can teach you right from wrong but I cannot always decide for you. I can buy you beautiful clothes but I cannot make you beautiful inside. I can offer you advice but I can't force you to accept it. I can give you love but I can't force it on you. I can teach you to share but I cannot make you unselfish. I can advise you about friends but I cannot choose them for you. I can advise you about sex but only you can build your reputation. I can tell you about drink and drugs but I can't say no for you. I can tell you about lofty goals but I can't achieve them for you. I can teach you kindness but really it's up to you to show it. I can tell you about sin but I can't make your morals. I can pray for you but I can't make you walk with God. I can tell you how to live, but in the end it's up to you.

 Notes

Orange Canvas: As we move towards September the skyline can often be transformed into an array of colour at sunset

AUGUST 30TH

'Men and women know that they have within themselves a ceaseless craving for satisfaction and completion which they do not and cannot find on Earth. It is this great something we call God.'
—Kevin Lyon

The great search for meaning, satisfaction and completion goes on for each person, not occasionally, but every single day of our lives. For those who can say they have found God does not mean that the search is over. It is ongoing and always will be. We can never say we know God fully. God is so much bigger than our humble understanding of God. But what a difference our humble understanding makes. It brings stability, meaning, foundation and satisfaction into our lives. Take it all away and we're left with so little. In fact we're probably left with nothing. Today I thank God for my humble understanding of God. I may not have all the answers, I may be struggling, I may be doing okay but at least I have something to hold on to which is infinitely better than nothing at all.

 Notes

Morning Stretch: A swan goes for a good stretch in shallow water

AUGUST 31ST

'Into each life some rain must fall. Some days must be dark and dreary.' ~J Longfellow

Rain clouds have a deeper spiritual meaning . For all of us some days are indeed dark and dreary. We simply can't avoid them. But we live in a culture of quick fixes which frequently uses the phrase 'Get over it.' Sadness is seen as something against the natural order and something that if present in our lives, we need to fix right away and get rid of it. It is never healthy to remain in sadness but it is always good to know how it affects us. Knowing that some days will be dark for all of us can help us to be more attuned to the presence of light in our lives. Jesus in our Gospels was not afraid to stand with people in their dark and sad moments. While others fled, Jesus remained. It was a clear reminder that brighter and more hopeful days would follow. They did and still do.

🖋 Notes

SEPTEMBER

Looking My Best: A colourful cockerel waiting to be sold at Millstreet Horse Fair

SEPTEMBER 1ST

'Most of life is routine, dull and grubby, but routine is the momentum that keeps each of us going.'
~Ben Nicholas

This week is the first week back to school after the summer holidays. For some children it is a very exciting time and their parents as they begin school for the first time. For others they have made the transition to secondary school and begin a whole new journey. Traffic also gets back to its normal crazy levels again, particularly in the morning! For nearly everyone it is good to be back to a routine again. Routine allows us to be comfortable with what we have to do and what we like to do. Stress levels rise when the list of things we have to do becomes unmanageable. As we begin our journey through this month of September we ask God's blessings on all of us. We ask God to help us with our daily routine. We pray that we will get through all those necessary things we have to do and also to help us find the time for those things that we enjoy as well.

 Notes

Windmill Silhouette: A windmill on a hill stands out against the vibrant colours of a September sunset

SEPTEMBER 2ND

'A baby's chuckle, a child's laugh, a parent's love, birds in flight, fish in shoals, atoms spinning, stars sparkling, brains working, spirits soaring, a blade of grass, a luscious flower, a weed? Let these miracles do their work. Let these dime-a-dozen miracles free us from our prisons of incredulity' ~Tom Cahill

We often confine miracles to holy places, like Lourdes, Knock and Fatima. Even in these places miracles seem to be infrequent and rare. But are they? It all depends on what a miracle might mean to us. If we're expecting something spectacular and almost impossible then we are going to be disappointed. But if we understand a miracle as God's intervention, no matter how small, then miracles are plentiful and are to be found everywhere. Despite an onslaught of negative news all around us, there are miracles bubbling everywhere. God's creation and evolution is endless. We are a part of it. It's all around us. But we can miss it all through apathy, worry, stress, busy lifestyles and other distractions. These miracles are all around us, plentiful, endless and there to be enjoyed and celebrated.

 Notes

Sheltered Harbour: Kinsale looking its best in September sunshine

SEPTEMBER 3RD

'What would the world be like if you really knew the future? What if you knew it as you know the past? It would be the greatest horror. Imagine a life without surprises, it would be unlivable.'
~Donagh O'Shea

We have a fascination with the future. Fortune tellers, psychic readers and futurologists have never been busier. But even they can't tell everything, and snippets of what might happen can either console or terrify us. We plan for the future as best we can but it can never become our only focus. Every day brings its share of joys and setbacks, surprises and disappointments, blessings and moments to forget. We work through each day to the best of our abilities. We need support and encouragement each day. Some days are tough and difficult. Many are ordinary and good in their own way. It is in the ordinariness of each day that God meets us best. God's message throughout scripture is: "I will be with you next week, next month, next year but I am especially with you right now, in the beauty or darkness of this present moment. It is the only moment that matters."

 Notes

Collection Of Raindrops: An early morning shower transforms these fuchsia flowers

SEPTEMBER 4TH

'People will let us down, people are flawed and selfish and so are we. Welcome to humanity, now get over yourself and try and make it a better humanity by being a better human being yourself.'
~Garry O'Sullivan

We waste much time and energy complaining and giving out about people who don't live up to our expectations. We expect so much more and they leave us down badly. For some this experience may be really personal and hurtful. For others it may be quite general but there is still that feeling of being let down. But if we were to opt out of every formal and informal relationship that let us down, we'd be permanently on our own. We can't lose hope just because others let us down. They will do so again and we will also do it to others. We have to live with the roses and the warts. Our Gospels are a collection of stories about many people who had been let down, some over a long period of time. Jesus encouraged each to get up and get going again. He also encourages each of us to do the same and gives us a new sense of life, purpose and beginning.

 Notes

Colourful Family: It's amazing what you can do with some stones and a bit of paint!!

SEPTEMBER 5TH

Bits and Pieces… –Author Unknown

Stop trying to love God and let God love you. Don't stay away from your local church because there are so many hypocrites going. There's always room for one more! No person can be a friend of Jesus who is not a friend of their neighbour. The Church is not made up of people who are better than the rest, but of people who want to become better than they are. The day a person is Baptised is far more important than the day when a person is Ordained a priest or bishop. A child is not likely to find a father in God, unless they find something of God in their own father first. Success in marriage is more than finding the right person; it is being the right person. God wants spiritual fruit not spiritual nuts. Marriage is like a twirling baton or turning handsprings or eating with chopsticks. It looks easy until you try it. You grow up the day you have your first laugh at yourself.

 Notes

Total Concentration: David O'Sullivan from Coláiste Choilm is totally focused during a hurling game in Ballincollig, Co.Cork

SEPTEMBER 6TH

'Opportunity only knocks once' ~Old Proverb

An artist watched children sailing a boat at the water's edge, as the sun was setting at the end of a perfect day. There was something about the scene that touched the artist's soul and he wanted to capture the moment on canvas to have for posterity. But the artist had promised to meet a friend and the last bus was about to leave the seaside resort and he didn't want to be late for his appointment. He met his friend but the haunting beauty of the boat scene stayed with him. He returned the following evening but the sunset wasn't so colourful and no children were playing with their boat. The tragedy of life is so often the tragedy of the missed opportunity. I can let them slip by or I can seize them and give thanks to God for these precious moments.

 Notes

A hidden treasure: Connemara in Co.Galway is unique with warm soft colours transforming the landscape

SEPTEMBER 7TH

The following has been written by a fifth-year student and it's called 'Prayer in my life'

When I was a child my parents taught me how to pray. At first I learned the 'Our Father'. At that time I did not realise the great effect that this prayer would have on my life. I particularly remember my Confirmation. Although it was a long time ago I know it was a turning point in my life. I realised that God was not a myth or a man in the sky but rather a very real energy in the world. I didn't feel alone anymore. I pray best when I am being artistic in drama or through craftwork. God speaks to me in the enjoyment I get from this creativity. I truly believe that I would not survive without God. God is the love and beauty that I find in my life. Sometimes I don't pray as much as I should and I feel empty inside. I feel sad that some people cannot find God. God is a feeling that can never be taken from us, a feeling called love. I pray because I need the warmth that God gives to me each day.

 Notes

Basket Of Colour: A colourful basket in particulary eye-catching at Union Hall, West Cork

SEPTEMBER 8TH

'Our birthdays are feathers in the broad wing of time.' ~Jean Richter

The birthday of Mary is celebrated today. We don't know for certain when she was born but for nearly 1,500 years her birthday has been celebrated on September 8th. Every birthday is worthy of celebration and even more so when it comes to Mary. As the mother of God she is hugely popular. It is estimated that her prayer, Hail Mary is said two billion times every day across the world. For many years there has been a shocking denial in the role of women in all things spiritual. As a result many have walked away, unhappy, disheartened and fed up with the way they have been ignored and pushed to one side. This situation is very slowly changing, thanks no end to a fresh and deeper appreciation of Mary. Every birthday is our way of saying, "You are special, there's only one of you, we are happy that you exist." Today is our way of saying to Mary that we are happy that she has an important part to play in our lives. We invite her nurturing presence and compassionate love into all we do each day.

 Notes

No Getting Through: A web between clumps of heather stands out in morning sunshine

SEPTEMBER 9TH

'Of what use is it to search for God in holy places if I have lost God in my heart?' ~Kenneth Payne

So often when it comes to the really important and essential things in life, we are simply searching in the wrong places. The same goes for everything connected with God. Our search for God has to begin from within. If we are open to beginning or exploring a link with God, we will begin a journey with great potential. But this journey can only begin at home with myself, before it can happen anywhere else. Am I searching for God in the wrong place? Every journey has to have a beginning and the beginning of a spiritual journey must begin from the heart.

 Notes

Last Ferry Home: A ferry sets out for Whiddy Island from Bantry, Co.Cork

SEPTEMBER 10TH

'Let go. Why do you cling to pain? There is nothing you can do about the wrongs of yesterday. It is not yours to judge. Why hold on to the very thing which keeps you from hope and love?' ~Leo Buscaglia

I have had the privilege of journeying with different groups of students from Coláiste Choilm on pilgrimage/retreat days to Gougane Barra in West Cork. Part of the many gentle invitations extended to these young people and indeed anyone who visits Gougane Barra is to pick up a stone. The stone represents all that is difficult in our lives and those burdens that we all carry around with us. The invitation is 'let some of them go' and instead to invite God's healing, hope and love into our lives in place of all the negative stuff. During the day everyone is given the chance to get rid of these stones by throwing them into one of the many streams around Gougane Barra. To 'let go' is a positive spiritual exercise. Letting go is not to regret the past but to grow and live for the future. Letting go is to fear less and love more. It is something we all could do every now and again.

 Notes

A Watchful Eye: A deer keeps a close eye on proceedings in Doneraile Park, Co.Cork

SEPTEMBER 11TH

'There is a time to stand up for what we believe in, a time to be prophetic, a time to draw a line in the sand and a time to point out differences. But there is also a time to embrace across differences, to recognise that we can love and respect each other, even when we don't hold the same values.'
--Ronald Rolheiser

The Book of Ecclesiastes in the Old Testament reminds us that there is a time and a place for everything in life. It is a beautifully balanced outlook on life. It recognises that life never stands still and is constantly changing. Yet within all this change and movement, we can still make time for what really matters. Sometimes this means being firm, strong and resolute. It also means acceptance of difference. It means embracing other viewpoints which we may not agree with. Maybe a better word to sum it all up is flexibility. Am I flexible enough to enjoy all that God has given to me? Am I flexible enough to know that God's flexibility knows no bounds? It goes well beyond our own limited horizons.

 Notes

'Famous Five' Julieanne Martin, Fiona Ryan, Gillian O'Brien, Victoria St.Ledger and Jennifer Tobin are all smiles on their graduation from Coláiste Choilm in Silver Springs Moran Hotel, Cork

SEPTEMBER 12TH

'We do what we have to do because God has called us' ~ from 'A Breath Of Fresh Air' by Vincent Travers

He was well known in the village where he lived as 'the veggie man'. Each day he would push his cart, full of fresh fruit and vegetables, through the narrow streets that made up his rounds. On the cart, next to the cash box, he had a notebook. One day while serving a customer, the notebook fell to the ground, unnoticed by the veggie man. Later two children on their way home from school found the notebook. Thinking they had found something valuable, they opened it and started reading. It was not what they expected. Page after page contained memos: "Don't forget the poor family on the hill." "Ask Mary Jo about her ailing mother." "Check the house for the homeless. Make sure it is well supplied." "Say hello to old Mike," and so on. But written on the front page were the words: We do what we have to do, because God has called us. These words were the driving force behind everything he did and said. His vision was rooted in Gospel values. It can be our vision too.

 Notes

No Room For Error: A stuntman flies at speed from a ramp at Curraheen Park, Bishopstown, Cork

SEPTEMBER 13TH

A film called 'Goal'...

It is the story about a young player from Mexico who was trying to get a break and make it into Newcastle Football Club. The film gives some insight into the rough and tough side of football. At reserve level the young player wouldn't pass the ball when he should. The coach pulled him aside and asked him to run to the end of the pitch. He kicked the ball ahead of him. The coach repeated this and then asked the young player what he had learned. The player was unsure. The coach told him: "The ball will always be quicker than you. You will never be faster than it. So pass, pass and keep passing." Life has little place for solo runs. We do best working together and as a team. The same goes with our belief in God. It can never be a private affair or a solo run. Each of us can make our relationship with God as personal as we want but it only has real meaning in how we relate with others. We need each other for support and encouragement. It can never happen if we insist on going solo.

 Notes

At The Foot Of The Cross: This cross is the centre feature behind the altar in the Reconciliation Chapel, at Knock Shrine, Co.Mayo

SEPTEMBER 14TH

'Veneration is not and should not be escapism. To venerate the cross of Jesus we see our own cross. By looking upon it we do not run away. God moves out towards humanity in an act of love and humility. To venerate the cross links our suffering to that of Jesus and so to get caught up in that moment of salvation.' ~Michael Shorthall

Today is the Feast of the Veneration of the Cross. The cross is something so many people can identify with in their own lives. It shatters the notion of a comfortable God, having all the perks, taking it nice and easy and somehow outside our world and lives. Nothing could be further from the truth. The cross pulls God right into the middle of our struggles and into the sometimes mess of our own lives. We all have our struggles, setbacks, pain and suffering. Life doesn't or can't protect us from them. Today is a day to acknowledge our own cross whatever it might be or perhaps the difficult cross some person or family may be carrying right now. We ask God's help to give us strength, courage and hope to carry whatever cross we may be carrying right now.

 Notes

Simple But Effective: A fisherman uses a simple stick as a fishing rod out in Kenmare Bay

SEPTEMBER 15TH

Stumbling Block or Stepping Stone?

You are a stumbling block when you are unkind or unjust in the way you treat others. But you are a stepping stone when you support me and others in moments of weakness and doubt. You are a stumbling block when you keep me down, hold me back or make me inferior. But you are a stepping stone when you help me to believe in myself and boost my self confidence. You are a stumbling block when you exclude me or ignore me. But you are a stepping stone when you help me to grow and develop my potential. You are a stumbling block when you criticise me, sour me with cynicism and destroy my dreams. But you are a stepping stone when you understand and listen to me and accept me as I am. In our Gospels, Jesus was very much aware of the many stumbling blocks that we all face. But whenever he found them he always made sure to put stepping stones as well. What stepping stones do I need today and during the week? Can I be a stepping stone for someone?

 Notes

'Best Foot Forward!' The Junior Camóige team from Coláiste Choilm, Ballincollig putting their best foot forward in style at the start of a school blitz final

SEPTEMBER 16TH

'What can I do? Repeat that question. Trust that you, one person, can do for God what otherwise would not be done. You choose because you are chosen. You choose because in the heart of your desire to love, you have found the heart of God searching for you.' –from Come Follow Me

It is comforting and reassuring to know that God is always searching for us, looking out for us and importantly always on our side. For many people the presumption is often that God has given up on them. Perhaps it is the direction their life has taken, mistakes made, life struggles and disappointments or a combination of all together. But God is always on our side. Even if we choose a 100, 1,000 or even a million wrong options God will not abandon us. A normal human response will be, "Sure that's crazy. Why would God want to bother with me?" But God does. God's love for us goes way beyond our limited horizons. God always want to make us number one.

 Notes

Catching The Evening Sun: A colourful Monbritia flower catches some evening sunshine

SEPTEMBER 17TH

A bit of light humour . . . .

Why did the farmer bury all his money in his fields? He wanted rich soil! How do you make seven even? Take away the s! Have you heard about the restaurant on the moon? Great food but no atmosphere! Why did the woman wear a helmet at the dinner table? She was on a crash diet! What's an eight letter word that has only one letter in it? An envelope. What is the longest word in the dictionary? Smiles, because it has a mile between the s's! What's the hardest thing about falling out of the bed? The floor! What kind of pet can you stand on? A carpet! Why didn't the musical instruments email each other? They preferred to write notes! How can you find a really cool website? Put your computer in the fridge! How does an elephant climb an oak tree? It sits on an acorn and waits until it grows!

 Notes

Giant Grass: Miscanthus grass growing as an energy crop at Tooreenbawn with Clara Mountain in the background

SEPTEMBER 18TH

'We can't always trust what we hear with our ears but we can always trust what we hear with our heart.' ~Author Unknown

The Songhai are an ethnic group from western Africa. A missionary was translating the Bible into Songhai. Unable to find a word for 'to believe', he asked a native how to translate it. The native thought for a second and said, "It means to hear with the heart." What a lovely translation. It's another way of saying that God speaks in a gentle voice. We live in a noisy world so much so that we are uncomfortable when we have silence. In such a noisy world it can sometimes be difficult to hear each other speak, not to mind hearing God! The invitation each day is to trust our inner voice and to trust that inner quiet voice of God who always wants to lead us in the right direction.

 Notes

Wedding Smiles: Triona Jump and Alan Carroll are all smiles in St.Colman's Church, Ballintotis, Co.Cork

SEPTEMBER 19TH

Creativity is not ultimately about public recognition or outstanding achievement. It's about self expression, about nurturing something into life and about the satisfaction this brings with it.'
~Ronald Ronheiser

It's good and important to be creative and it is not limited by age. By being creative we are open to possibility and to God's gentle presence in our lives. When we choose not be creative we can become stale, negative, cynical and lacking energy to do anything. We tend to see people who are creative as the people who achieve much in life and who are always in the public limelight. We often call these people celebrities. But this is only a tiny fraction of the story. Everyone can be creative and when we do we add something special to each day that God gives us. Creativity can be as simple as reading a book, gardening, baking bread, keeping a journal, going for a walk, texting a friend, coaching the local sports team, playing cards, keeping a diary, enjoying photography, praying, cycling, woodwork and so much more. It doesn't have to get recognition. If you enjoy doing it then you are creative and you add something special to each day that God gives to you.

 Notes

Bathtime: A duck has an early morning stretch and bath at Doneraile Park, Co.Cork

SEPTEMBER 20TH

'A theology professor once recommended that we read poetry. Why poetry? Because it says what cannot be said. Preachers have to talk constantly about God, whom they have never seen. Poets do not try to box up and parcel God. They possess the great charism of humility before God's awesome mystery.' ~Michael McGrath

Poetry is alive and well and not something confined to the past. Many poems continue to be written each day. Many of these never get published but are written to express something personal and important. Many of them are hidden gems. Poems that in some way refer to God are often uplifting, open and honest because they simply do not attempt to box up and parcel God. A mistake of formal religion is to sometimes put God in a box or parcel and then add on the gift paper ready made. It can't be done and can often be out of touch with the experience of people at ground level. Everyone's experience of God is different which is why we always need an approach that is open, fresh and liberating. Poets do it naturally and there is a poet in all of us.

 Notes

Time To Go Home: These surfers are happy to go home after some great surfing at Garretstown, Co.Cork

SEPTEMBER 21ST

'The theme of St.Matthew's writing is that faith is a shared experience. Our faith or lack of it affects others. We are therefore able to transmit spiritual energy to one another.' ~Joseph Krempa

Today is the Feast of St.Matthew. He was a tax collector and as a result people hated and despised him. As a result of his lifestyle, he was an outcast but yet Jesus saw beyond his role as a tax collector and knew that he had so much to give his expanding team. His feast day coincides with the autumn equinox, of equal light and darkness. Matthew himself was the writer of the first of the four Gospels and his Gospel highlights the equality that Jesus brought to everyone he met. For Matthew, every person was to be valued and respected for who they were. Everyone had a contribution to make, particularly at local level and for Matthew there were no exceptions. Today's feast day also challenges us in how we treat others. Do I treat people differently according to what they have, own or speak? We are encouraged to make as few distinctions as possible. It is never easy, but Matthew led the way.

 Notes

Vibrant Colours: A butterfly shows its true colours as it stretches on a flower

SEPTEMBER 22ND

'Once you begin to learn about yourself and begin to take yourself seriously, things begin to happen.' ~Gareth O'Callaghan

We are sometimes slow in believing in ourselves, slow in believing our potential and slow believing in the endless possibilities we can generate. Unless we first believe in ourselves we can never believe in anything else. Our world is complex, fragile and difficult at the best of times. In such a world we need to believe that there is something more. This something more can be different things but to many it simply is a belief in God, who loves us, cares for us and wants us to believe in the vast goodness and potential within. God always accepts us as we are but sadly many don't believe that God works this way. Today we can begin to believe that we have something significant and positive to bring to any day. It's not about how much but much more about each of us realising that we have far more than we realise.

 Notes

A Glimpse Of The Past; A blacksmith works with the furnace of his forge in Muckross Traditional Farm, Killarney,

SEPTEMBER 23RD

'Accept that there will always be those who will hold different beliefs and follow different paths to our own. Learn to respect people as they are and put differences aside.' ~Ronan Scully

Diversity has always been a part of our universe. Nature programmes are hugely successful because they explore such diversity among animals, birds and insects. When it comes to people, we tend to be slow to embrace difference and diversity. It is part of being human to want others to agree with our own viewpoint. Problems begin when we begin to impose our viewpoints onto somebody. We feel we're absolutely right, we know it's the only way and so should they! The challenge is to embrace different viewpoints and to accept that others, even those closest to us, will see things different from us. A prayer today is to ask God to help me understand that my story is important, but that there are other stories out there just as important and valuable.

 Notes

Bubble Reflections: Kim Broderick is reflected in a big bubble, thanks to lovely sunshine streaming into the science room at Coláiste Choilm, Ballincollig

SEPTEMBER 24TH

'It seems to have become increasingly acceptable to state that religion has no part to play in public life and that those with religious faith should keep their views to themselves.'
~Nuala O'Loan

Our faith is like a little stream. On its own it may seem insignificant but every stream has its own unique energy. It will soon link up with other streams, gathering momentum and a sense of purpose. No one can stop the flow of a stream. You can build a dam to stop it but the stream will fill, back up and flow over it. Its ultimate destination is the sea and nothing can stop it on its journey. The same goes with the gift of faith and what we believe in. It is something precious and unique. It can't be hidden or swept into some corner. It has an energy that drives it forward. It helps us on the journey of life to find meaning and fulfilment. It never does a solo run but joins and links up with people who share the same vision and hope. There are so many different faith stories across the world. Like streams and rivers the variety and number is breath taking. But they all flow into the one great ocean, that of an eternal loving God.

 Notes

Ripple Effect: A stone thrown into the water at Gougane Barra sends out ripples in all directions

SEPTEMBER 25TH

'The best remedy for those who are afraid, lonely or unhappy is to go outside, somewhere where they can be quiet, alone with the heavens, nature and God. I firmly believe that nature brings solace in all troubles.' ~Anne Frank

Today is the Feast of St.Finbarr. Gougane Barra is located a few miles west of Ballingeary,in west Cork, situated in a picturesque setting and it was here that Finbarr built his monastery in the 6th-century. Clearly Finbarr knew that God was very much present here, particularly in the beauty of nature that is evident all year round. Against a backdrop of rugged hills, lakes, rivers and streams, Finbarr found great peace. The Feast of St.Finbarr today reminds us how important it is to appreciate many things around us. Like the ripples in the water going out in all directions, so do our little contributions in life. Our contribution is always valued, respected and so important. Life moves so fast we could miss the impact of all our contributions in life. Today is a day of blessing and we ask the blessings of St.Finbarr on ourselves, our families, our schools, our communities, and those who need a special prayer today. May St.Finbarr continue to guide and direct us each day.

 Notes

Ready Steady Go!!: Thousands of women take off at the start of the Evening Echo Women's Mini Marathon

SEPTEMBER 26TH

'Consider the endless possibilities that our young people have within themselves and their genuine desire for God in their lives. It is these possibilities that bring about a hope that is lived out in every one of our young people today.' ~Patricia O'Brien

When it comes to young people the perception out there is that they have abandoned the faith, with little connection to God in their lives. All the evidence points to a much different story. Often it is the sceptic in us that doubts the motivation behind what a young person may do. We don't give them enough credit or try to understand where they are coming from. Many young people are genuinely searching for God and are willing to seek God out in their lives. This search may not always be obvious but it is alive and well. They need our support and encouragement on that journey.

 Notes

Ever So Close: Two jets from the Red Arrows come tantalisingly close at Salthill, Galway

SEPTEMBER 27TH

The Five Finger Prayer Guide:

(1) Your thumb is nearest you. So begin your prayers by praying for those closest to you. They are the easiest to remember.

(2) The next finger is the pointing finger. Pray for those who teach, instruct and heal. This includes teachers, doctors, nurses, counsellors, priests, sisters and others in the caring profession. They need support and wisdom in pointing others in the right direction. Keep them in your prayers.

(3) Next is the tallest finger. It reminds us of our leaders. Pray for our president, leaders in government, business and industry. These people shape our nation and guide public opinion. They need God's guidance.

(4) The fourth finger is our ring finger. Surprising to many is the fact that this is our weakest finger, as any piano teacher will testify. It should remind us to pray for those who are weak, in trouble or in pain. They need our prayers day and night.

(5) Lastly is our little finger, the smallest finger of all. Here we should place ourselves in relation to God and others. Your little finger should remind you to pray for yourself. You yourself know best your own needs and concerns.

 Notes

In Transition: Summer slowly gives way to autumn colour

SEPTEMBER 28TH

'God gives each of us one small piece of this earth, which we alone can make our own, during our span of life. We are called by God to make it blossom and bloom. If we opt out there is no question that God's work will go on.' ~Vincent Travers

Our patch may seem small and at times insignificant, but it is the most important of all. Our life patch will always bloom in God's own time and way. We can make it happen in lots of different ways, but it mainly happens when we're open to life and all the blessings it can bring. We bring with us our own uniqueness, our originality, our charm, our laughter and humour, our energy, our hopes and dreams and so much more. No one can take these from us. The gentle invitation each day is to use them to help our little patch blossom and bloom. The spotlight tends to be on negative news. We are bombarded and saturated with it. But today why not put the spotlight on your good news and the blossoms in your life?

 Notes

Sparkling Leaves: A beech tree in memory of Dan Callanan with sparkling red colours

SEPTEMBER 29TH

'I think children and indeed adults have the expectation that they have a right to be entertained. It is almost as if it is the government's fault that they are bored.' ~Antony Sutch

Why are so many people seemingly bored these days? Technology has created endless possibilities. You can store thousands of songs into a tiny ipod. Mobile phones are internet linked with access to any information we want. Yet it seems we are bored. The underlying cause must be deeper. There seems to be no connection today with anything spiritual in our lives. Spirituality connects us with something deeper and lasting. But sadly we are losing that connection. We don't know how to feed our minds and hearts with something substantial. But it's not too late to find ways and means that will bring our lives meaning and fulfilment. Am I bored with life? Am I looking for something deeper? Can I make a little room for God in my busy life?

 Notes

Happy Brides: These brides are all smiles after finishing the Women's Mini Marathon and raising lots of money for charity

SEPTEMBER 30TH

'People cultivate five thousand roses in one garden and still they do not find what they seek. Yet what they are seeking may be found in a single rose or a drop of water.' ~Antoine de Sainte-Exupery

Down through the years we've been led to believe in the numbers game. A consumerist society feeds into more and plenty of everything. The more you have the happier you'll be is the motto. But this is not always the case. Recent surveys have shown that people are not happier and that they seek lasting happiness. It is easy to believe that lots of everything will bring happiness when there is little else seemingly on offer. A close look at our Gospels indicates that happiness and contentment are actually within our grasp. The words used are 'finding the kingdom of God.' It is among us, around us and within our reach. One person, one gesture of love and kindness, one smile, one text, one word of encouragement can be enough to make it begin to happen. The power of one cannot be measured.

 Notes

OCTOBER

St.Therese: Photo was taken in St.Colman's Church, Macroom, Co.Cork

OCTOBER 1ST

'Our duty in this world is to help others by showing them their roses and not their thorns. Only then can we achieve the love we should feel for each other. Only then can we bloom in our garden.'
~Author Unknown

A story is told about a man who planted a rose and watered it faithfully and before it blossomed, he examined it. He saw the bud that would soon blossom and also the thorns. And he thought, "How can any beautiful flower come from a plant burdened with so many sharp thorns?" Saddened by this thought, he neglected to water the rose and before it was ready to bloom, it died. The same goes for each of us too. Unfortunately many of us look at ourselves and see only the thorns, our weak points and what's negative. We often do not see the rose within ourselves. St.Therese, whose feast day is today, is famous for her outlook on life. For Therese, great things can happen among the simple things in life and also among the thorns. Beyond every thorn, there is great beauty and potential. Sometimes we just have to make a bigger effort to see beyond those thorns.

 Notes

Profusion Of Colour: The walkway into the oratory of St.Finbarr at Gougane Barra is full of autumn colours

OCTOBER 2ND

'Everyone no matter how humble they may be has angels to watch over them. They are heavenly, pure and splendid. They have been given to keep us company on our way. They have been given the task of keeping careful watch over us.' ~Pope Pius XII

Today is the Feast of our guardian angel. We all have our own guardian angel and they are as influential as we allow them to be. The more we believe in them and call on them, the greater their presence and influence in our lives. Our guardian angel is always with us and is always ready to help, guide and direct us. Pope Pius is famous for devotion to his guardian angel and said that without such devotion he would never have got through all the delicate and difficult situations he often faced. Today is a day when we can pray to our personal guardian angel. It's not asking him/her to solve all of life's problems, but to simply be a beacon of light and hope along our own daily journey. Our guardian angel will never let us down.

 Notes

My Precious Bride: Joe Keane holding Tonya O'Mahony on the beach at La Cala de Mijas, Spain

OCTOBER 3RD

'What you put into life is what you get out of it.' ~Old Saying

At the start of October a Day for Life is celebrated. It came as a response to the proposal of the late Pope John Paul II that a Day for Life be celebrated to foster in ourselves, in families, in our community, in civil society, a recognition of the meaning and value of human life. Sadly we hear many tragic stories on a daily basis, from murders, rape, physical assaults, exploitation and so on. Life is often crushed and destroyed. We know of people who find life itself a struggle, caught in the web of depression and deep loneliness. What's the point of a Day for Life? It is a day for us to appreciate our own life and life all around us. We take so much for granted, especially life. It is fragile, delicate and there is great beauty to be found when someone bubbles with life. Our prayer today is asking God to help us nurture and treasure life but especially to pray for those whom for life is an uphill struggle.

 Notes

Crossing Over: Tourists cross the bridge on the upper section of the Gap of Dunloe, near Killarney

OCTOBER 4TH

'When criticism seems unfair, I believe it helps to remember the hawk. When attacked by crows, it does not counterattack. Instead, the hawk soars higher and higher in ever widening circles until the pests leave it alone.' ~Steve Goodier

We often take criticism personally. Some criticism is unfair and can be a put-down. But some criticism can also be for our own good. When someone is critical they often forget to mention the positive and good points as well! What a difference it would make if they did. Like the hawk we too sometimes need to circle wide of personal attacks when they become bitter and nasty. When we circle wide we are not sucked into a counterattack that drains our energy and confidence. Jesus himself sometimes moved away to a quiet spot. It was not running away but simply put him in a better position on his return to deal with opposition, friction and criticism.

 Notes

Let's Celebrate: Clonakilty celebrate after winning the Cork County football final

OCTOBER 5TH

'There must be more to life than having everything.' ~Maurice Sendak

Thomas Aquinas probably answers it best when he said that whenever we speak about God there is only one thing we can be sure of, that we're wrong! Any attempt to speak about God can never be too far wrong though if we say that God is love. The Trinity is about the relationship of Father, Son and Holy Spirit. We have heard the saying that two is company but three is a crowd. Three is a number that occurs regularly in the Gospels: three wise men, Jesus tempted three times in the desert, Peter denied Jesus three times, Jesus fell three times on the road to Calvary, three days in the tomb and so on. While we may not fully be able to explain the mystery of the Trinity it is good to acknowledge that much of life is a mystery. Life can be unpredictable, uncertain and at times cruel. In the mystery of life we believe that God is somewhere in the middle, helping us to cope and adapt. Somewhere in the middle of it all are three forces working together as one and hopefully making a difference to all our lives.

 Notes

Unique Hairstyle: An alpaca gets lots of attention with its eye-catching hairdo at Ballinagree Show, Co.Cork

OCTOBER 6TH

'The amazing thing about prayer is that it equally helps the pray-er and the pray-ee. Maybe if we were charged a fee to pray we would have a better sense of its value. Of course, no-one could afford it, for the value of prayer is priceless' –Vickie Girard

There has been much written and said about prayer. The one common link with anyone sharing their thoughts on prayer is its great benefits. There is no denying the difficulties either. It's easy to go into a shop, buy what you want and see immediate results for what you buy. If only the same could be said of prayer. Prayer is so much different. Results are not immediate and obvious. But prayer is never a waste of time and every attempt to connect with God does bring a blessing that no money can buy. Each prayer firmly grounds us in the present moment. When we pray we bring whatever is going on in our lives. Sometimes it's good and upbeat. Sometimes it's ugly, desperate and dark. But God never judges any prayer, but accepts us as we are. The real value of every prayer is to know that God is very much on our side.

 Notes

I Can Carry Everything!:A black labrador is full of life and energy at Salthill, Galway

OCTOBER 7TH

'Will the real you please stand up, please stand up, please stand up.' ~Eminem

As we journey through life we change. Simple things like fashion are interesting. Most people laugh when they see pictures of themselves five or ten years ago. Our taste in music may change as do our opinions, our goals, our ambitions and our hopes for tomorrow. This is good and healthy. Sometimes we need to have the courage to cast off the layers of identity that we thought was us but actually isn't. Another way of putting it is to allow the real you or me stand up. Jesus criticized the Pharisees and Scribes because everything about them was so false. They were afraid of themselves. Jesus simply says: 'Be yourself'. The challenge for us is to be authentic. It's about letting the real you stand up. It's about being honest with ourselves each day including our feelings. The easy option is to retreat, to be afraid and hide but the Gospel call is to let the real you stand up.

 Notes

My Hiding Place: A duck partially hides in the reeds on the river Blackwater

OCTOBER 8TH

'A candle flame has a fascination for people of all ages. It is a kind of living thing; it breathes the air and drinks the molten wax to nourish its life. Though it stirs occasionally like a sleeping baby, it lives mostly in silent contemplation.' ~Ned Grace

A candle can represent many different things for people. A candle is comforting, consoling, uplifting and can be a sign of great hope, particularly during a difficulty or crisis. The candle can also represent people who live quiet lives. These people may not grab the headlines and may not do anything seemingly extraordinary. Yet these people are truly inspirational. They may be quiet in the background but their value and importance can never be measured. Big strong spotlights are prone to breaking down and giving up at the wrong time. But you can always rely on the safe and steady light of a candle. Even in total darkness, the light of a candle is truly extraordinary. Today is a day to thank God for those people in our lives who mirror a candle, quiet and gently getting on with what needs to be done. These people continue to inspire, nurture and bless us all.

 Notes

Exotic Sunset: The skyline is a dazzling display of colour at La Cala de Mijas in Spain

OCTOBER 9TH

'Optimism is faith in our own efforts and in human potentiality. It is in God however that we place our hope. Hope does not deny the pain and suffering of the present. Rather it courageously faces up to this, stays with the pain but refuses to be enslaved by it and at the appropriate time, is prepared to move forward.' ~Michael Neary

We sometimes confuse optimism with hope. Optimism relies on the human person. It requires courage, willpower, bravery and a belief that things will improve. However we are fragile and weak. Sometimes our initial optimism quickly fades. Hope on the other hand has its roots in God. We put our hope and trust in God. Hope is not a protective shield from the knocks of the world and life. Hope will always allow us to take a step forward away from darkness, despair, confusion and hopelessness. A combination of optimism and hope is one that will never let us down. We pray to God to help us to be optimistic and hopeful, particularly when it is difficult to be so.

 Notes

Ripe And Ready: Apples ready for picking

OCTOBER 10TH

'Maybe we can only recognise the beauty surrounding us when we welcome the beauty that lies deep within us. The sadness is that we become so busy and bothered about the trials and difficulties that beset us that we seldom give time to welcome this gift' ~Far East Magazine

One of the great spiritual writers, St Paul wrote a lovely letter to the Philippians and asked them to think about things around them that were true, lovely and gracious (Phil 4:8). At the time of writing this letter, life was tough and difficult for many of them-including Paul. But he saw the importance of looking at the bigger picture and particularly the great beauty that lies within each person. There is much darkness, sadness and negativity in the world we live in but it should never cloud or block out all the good and positive within each person. Sometimes to appreciate this precious gift we need to concentrate on something that is life-giving for us. Maybe it's a summer flower in your garden, maybe a painting, a poem, a pet, a piece of music or a favourite album. The poet Patrick Kavanagh said he encountered his beautiful God every time he went to the boglands. It was a sacred place for him and it was life-giving. What place for me is life-giving? What do I like doing that is also life giving? What person energises and brings me life? God is at the heart of all that is life-giving.

 Notes

Autumn Colours: This beech tree is rich in colour

OCTOBER 11TH

There are many ways of saying 'Well done'.........

That's great, Super, That's good, You are brilliant at that, That's coming along nicely, That's the best you have ever done, You're doing a really good job, What an improvement, I knew you could do it, Congratulations, I couldn't have done it better myself, Nice going, You haven't missed anything, Wow, Keep up the good work, Terrific, Nothing can stop you now, That's the way to do it, Sensational, That's the best ever, Wonderful, You have done that so well, Nice one, Outstanding, Fantastic, Tremendous, Now that's what I call a fine job, You certainly did well today, Keep it up, You did a lot of work today, I really appreciate what you have done, I'd be lost without you, You're one in a million, You really are an inspiration, Thank you so much, Marvellous, You're a star, May God bless you for all you've done. There may be many ways of saying well done, but the most important of them all is the one you actually say to someone.

 Notes

My Perch: A fly lands on the petal of a fuchsia flower

OCTOBER 12TH

'Awe and wonder are experienced whenever we sense the sacred, and most of the time, this is the humdrum of daily living.' ~Author Unknown

If one is lucky enough to live in the country or if one can get away from the light pollution of towns and cities, it is possible on a clear night to see thousands of stars. The Milky Way, the galaxy in which we live, is made up of billions of stars and our galaxy is only one of billions of galaxies! Our universe is mind-boggling huge. It has the awe and wonder factor of which we are a tiny part. But that tiny part is probably the most important part of all. Perhaps wonder and awe today have been replaced by cynicism and fear but nothing can replace our importance within the bigger story. God is to be found in the great and small but when we look for God in the small and semingly mundane things of everyday life, we will not be disappointed.

 Notes

Raindrop Collector: A spider's web becomes the collector of many raindrops after a heavy dew

OCTOBER 13TH

'Love is such an overused word. Pop songs sing about love. Everything revolves around love. Many people only connect love with the idea of fulfilled sexuality. But however much the word is misused, in the depths of our heart everyone longs for love.' –Anselm Gruen

We all know someone special who radiates love. It is not an act, or something put on. They radiate it naturally and it simply flows from them. Everyone has the ability to do this but for different reasons the flow becomes blocked. It might be a hurt, a knock or setback in life. Someone may have betrayed our trust. We may have been taken advantage of or we may have grown afraid because others hurt us in the past. Scripture readings refer to God as love. This is 100% pure natural divine love. It is total, complete and will never run out. Each day is an invitation to soak in some of this love. The invitation is to allow it melt away our hurts, fears, anxieties, disappointments or darkness in our lives. Every time we take up this invitation allows us to radiate our own love naturally. No matter what our age, our belief system or our background, this is what we are born to do.

 Notes

Mission: A beautiful piece of artwork put together by Rang Clár is the centre feature in the prayer room at Coláiste Choilm, Ballincollig to mark Mission Week

OCTOBER 14TH

'Mission is always looking outwards, reaching out beyond ourselves, our home, our community, our parish, our diocese, our nation. Mission is opening oneself to others as brothers and sisters, discovering and encountering them, sharing their joys and suffering' —Intercom Magazine

Each year the focus is put on mission during the month of October. We often think of missionaries as just priests and sisters but we also include many people who take time out and who have decided to give some months or longer to work with the underprivileged in various parts of the world. 80% of the world's population lives in poverty, so the challenges are extensive. Mission is all about celebrating the work of missionaries, remembering them in our prayers and asking God's blessings on all the good work they do. Mission is not about having all the answers. It is embracing and respecting so many different beliefs and viewpoints about God. Mission celebrates the uniqueness of every single person, no matter what their beliefs. We pray today for all our missionaries.

 Notes

Powerdive: A white tailed sea eagle powers off to safety with its catch of the day!

OCTOBER 15TH

'I invite you to pray for those with mental health difficulties, that they are not placed on the margins but treated with respect and lovingly supported as they live their life with dignity.' ~Pope Benedict XVI

One in four people will experience a mental health problem at some stage in their life. Good mental health helps us to enjoy life and to face disappointments, pain and sadness which we will all inevitably experience at some stage. The effects of mental illness can be deep and painful. One can lose a sense of direction and control in our lives. It can lead to isolation and loneliness. In dealing with mental health we are slow to talk about problems, especially men. There is an assumption that no-one will understand my pain. When we talk about our negative feelings we give ourselves permission to take one step forward. The good news is that the majority of people with a mental illness get better or learn to manage their symptoms in daily life. We pray today for anyone affected by a mental illness and we pray especially for healing. The Samaritans can be contacted on 1850 609090

 Notes

Walking On Shadows: A pedestrian walking along a colourful Great William O'Brien Street, Blackpool, Cork

OCTOBER 16TH

'Real generosity is doing something nice for someone who will never find out.' ~ Frank A.Clark

How do you describe a generous person? One explanation is someone who is warm-hearted and who delights in ensuring the happiness and welfare of others. In Irish there is one single word that sums it all up and it's to be flaithiúlacht. There are many examples where God is generous or flaithiúlacht. In the wedding at Cana, Jesus asks that the jars be filled with water but goes a step further by saying, 'fill them to the brim'. In another story a huge number of fish are caught by the disciples who had given up on catching any. The fish are so many that the nets begin to tear and extra boats are called to help. God is lavish, generous and flaithiúlacht. When we think we least deserve God's generosity is the moment when God is most generous.

 Notes

Electric Red: A red leaf stands out in October sunshine

OCTOBER 17TH

Ten Spiritual Tips for today...

(1) Stop worrying. Worry kills life. (2) Begin each day with a prayer. It will arm your soul. (3) Control appetite. Over indulgence clogs mind and body. (4) Accept your limitations. There are few who are great and they have enough worries. (5) Don't envy. It wastes times and energy. (6) Have faith in people. Cynicism is caustic. (7) Exercise. Go for a walk. Get out and about. It clears the mind. (8) Read a book to stimulate imagination and broaden your views. (9) Spend some time alone for the peace and solitude of silence. (10) Try to want what you have instead of spending your strength trying to get what you want.

 Notes

Kiss For Mum: Rosemary Daly gets a big kiss from her daughter Tara, on her wedding day

OCTOBER 18TH

'Taking responsibility for oneself and one's actions is required for true happiness. Don't be given to blaming others for your faults, mistakes and misfortunes. They are yours, take responsibility for them, while trying to lessen and avoid them in the future. Appreciate your talents and achievements and be grateful for them. Count your blessings. This is clearly an inside job. Only you can do it.'
~ Bill Cosgrave

What lovely words of wisdom. So often we look to others and other things for happiness but it can only begin with ourselves. Taking responsibility for the choices we make is often easier said than done. We are often influenced by peer pressure, by the expectations of others, by clever and seductive advertising and by expecting too much of ourselves. While our life circumstances may change, while ill health, unemployment or financial struggles may dominate, we must always have a positive attitude about ourselves. Any search for happiness requires a first step and that step will always be appreciating and feeling good about oneself. If it's not there we are trying to climb a wall and then a cliff. At the heart of our Gospel stories Jesus helped every single person take that first step. It was often life-changing, liberating and a new beginning. Nothing has changed today. Are you comfortable in taking that first step?

 Notes

Evolution Of Colour: A tree is transformed into dazzling autumn colour

OCTOBER 19TH

'Priorities are not written in granite. They need to be flexible and change as we do. I find it helpful to think of priorities as the wooden frame upon which we stretch the canvas of our days.' ~Sarah Breathnach

A priority is something that is important to each of us. Our health is an important priority, as is the welfare of our family, financial security, employment and so on. There are many other priorities that are unique to each of us. For some the main priority is simply to get through this day. We are indeed pulled in all directions and it's sometimes hard to know what's important and what takes priority. The image of the wooden frame is helpful and particularly when we apply it to God. Each day is God's precious gift to us and like a canvas it is blank, waiting for us to add our colour. If we don't prioritise certain things we end up trying to do everything and in the end have little to show for it. What one thing is important to me today? Can I do something to make it happen?

 Notes

Day 293

Falling Down: A chimney is all on its own, with lots of colour all around it

OCTOBER 20TH

A reflection written by an older person:

Old age, I decided, is a gift. I am now probably for the first time in my life, the person I have always wanted to be. Oh, not my body. I sometimes despair over the wrinkles and the baggy eyes! But not for long as I would never trade my amazing friends, my wonderful life, my loving family for one less grey hair or a flatter belly. As I've aged, I've become more kind to myself and less critical. I've become my own friend. I have seen too many dear friends leave this world too soon before they understood the great freedom that comes with ageing. What does it matter if I read until two and sleep until noon? I know I am sometimes forgetful. But then again, some of life is just as well forgotten. Sure, over the years my heart has been broken. I've been through tough times and broken hearts are what give us understanding and compassion. As you get older, it is easier to be positive. You care less about what other people think and I've earned the right to be wrong. So I like being old. It has set me free. I like the person I have become. I am not going to live forever and with God's help I'm going to make the most of every day that's left.

 Notes

We Did It!: Marie Neville, Róisín McCarthy and Muirgen O'Mahony from Coláiste Choilm are in great form after winning another game at Ballincollig

OCTOBER 21ST

'I want to be a great saint but I also want to experience all the sensations that sinners have. I want to spend long hours in prayer but I don't want to miss anything on television.' ~Henri Nouwen

Everyone struggles to keep life simple and straight-forward. Quite simply we want everything and we simply can't have it. One of the great saints of simplicity is St.Therese. When she was seven years old, one of her older sisters Leonie decided that it was time for her to give up her toys. So she gathered them all up into a big box. She then told Therese that she could only choose one thing from the box and that the rest were going to charity. Apparently Therese froze and was unable to choose. She simply said: "I choose them all. I want them all!" All the great spiritual writers and indeed the scriptures remind us that it's hard to find God when we want everything. We tend to be distracted and focussed elsewhere. No wonder life can be trying and tiring. Life isn't simple and it never will be. We need to respect its complexity and our complexities. But that should never stop us from trying to live and enjoy the simpler things in life. It is in simple, ordinary, down to earth moments that we will find greater fulfilment, meaning and purpose.

 Notes

Nature's Masterpiece: A beech tree is full of colour despite a shower of rain

OCTOBER 22ND

Often in the evening, I reflect on the people I have met that day. I remember them in prayer, aware of life moving, changing and growing. Time, though fragile and passing seems to have an eternal dimension. One evening I wrote: 'Time stands still here, a time beyond the daily chime or ticking of the clock, a rhythm in tune, with eternity.' – Patricia Byrne

Time for the most part seems to go by quickly. We plan lots of things in any given day and time allows us to do only so much. Sometimes when we plan better, we can push to one side activities that eat time and are not life giving. We can concentrate on those things that really matter, those things that need priority and importantly, give us energy and life. Putting such a plan in place is easier said than done, but the benefits are impressive and noticeable. It is also so healthy and wise to recall at the end of each day those moments where time seemed to stand still. It was a moment that was special and one that we would have liked to stay in. Time pushed us on but in recalling the beauty of that moment later, we are in some sense in touch with eternity. In recalling one or more of those moments at the end of any day, is in fact a beautiful prayer to God.

 Notes

Jazzing It Up: A jazz band gets everyone at Coláiste Choilm in the mood for the Cork Jazz Festival

OCTOBER 23RD

'Our world has grown weary of greed, exploitation and division. Humanity is squandering the Earth's resources to satisfy its insatiable appetite for material goods.'
~Pope Benedict speaking at the World Youth Day

There is nothing like direct words and more so when they speak the truth. Our world as we know it is at a crossroads. It can only be exploited and depleted of all its natural gifts and resources for so long. It is at the point of exhaustion. The Pope in speaking to such a large gathering of young people has his finger very much on the pulse of life. It is these young people who can make the difference, who can bring about change and who can begin to make things happen. It can be easy to be dismissive, negative and pessimistic. It can be easy to call it hype and wide of the mark. But we as a generation, are doing our best to destroy everything that's been given to us. We as a generation must play our part to turn things around.

 Notes

Club Colours: A car is painted in the Carraig na bhFear club colours in support of its local GAA team

OCTOBER 24TH

'There are two ways of spreading light; to be the candle or the mirror that reflects it.' ~Edith Wharton

There is a story about a man who was abroad on work commitments in France. He bought a rock that intrigued him. It looked ordinary but the shopkeeper showed him how each of the cracks in the rock would shine with different coloured lights in the dark. The businessman bought it for his wife as a symbol of their love and packed it away in his suitcase. On returning home some weeks later he asked his wife to turn out the lights, took out the rock and gave it to his wife. But nothing happened. The man was upset, "I've been cheated and I paid a lot of money for this." He explained to his wife that he had bought the rock as a symbol of his love for her and that each crack on the rock was supposed to glow with a different coloured light in the dark. She graciously accepted the rock, put it back in its box and kissed him lovingly. Next day she took the box to her neighbour to translate the French words on the side of the box. "It's a simple instruction", said the neighbour, "If you want me to shine in the dark, expose me to the sunlight." Because he had kept the rock in his suitcase it couldn't shine. The rock can be symbolic of many things in our lives. Spiritually it means we remain in the dark until we turn towards God, the greatest source of light and energy in our world.

Tied Up: Two boats and beautiful autumn colours set the scene for a picture postcard view of Gougane Barra, west Cork

OCTOBER 25TH

'I have come so that you may have life and have it to the full' ~ John's Gospel 10:10

The above line can be a great starter for prayer. The following little prayer is one such start: 'Lord, you don't give anything away in half measures but always complete and full. Your offer of life to us is touching and inspiring. Help me to appreciate that you are the greatest source of life and energy in our world today. Help me to live life to the full and in doing so experience your life and blessings in my life. Even when it seems that the floodwaters and storms are closing in on me, help me to realize that you are always closer to me than I can possibly imagine. Thank you for your gentle presence in my life. Amen'

 Notes

'No Let Up' A young rider shows the sheer intensity and speed involved in show jumping at a competition held in Green Glens, Millstreet, Co.Cork

OCTOBER 26TH

'Hope grows. It rejoices and it struggles. Hope is challenged,but it never dies. It stumbles but it never falls. Hope is life and life is hope. It is always on the move but it is always there.' ~ Shauna Mongwanga

The core values of Christianity are faith, hope and love. All else evolves from these three together and none of them work on their own. We all know what hope is, but where does it come from and how does it apply to our lives? The source of our hope is in God who simply loves us and who can do nothing else. It's about a God who never stops seeking us and who never gives up on us. St.Paul wrote a lot about this and described it in a lovely way by saying: "Hope does not disappoint us because God's love has been poured into our hearts." Throughout this day we can be a sign of hope and inspiration to someone else. It often happens when we least expect and often we're not even aware it's happening.

 Notes

Standing Tall And Pretty: These Nerine flowers add a burst of colour to their background

OCTOBER 27TH

A prayer called the 'The Knots Prayer' ~Author Unknown

Dear God, Please untie the knots that are in my mind, my heart and life. Remove the have-not, the cannot and the do-not that I have in my mind. Erase the will not, may not and might not that may find a home in my heart. Release me from the could not, would not and should not that obstruct my life. And most of all dear God, I ask that you remove from my mind, my heart and my life all of the 'am nots' that I have allowed to hold me back, especially the thought that I am not good enough. Amen.

 Notes

Mum, I Can Do What You Are Doing!: A young calf gets its head in through a feeding barrier

OCTOBER 28TH

'Know that you are the perfect age. Each year is special and precious, for you shall only live it once.'
~Louise Hay

It's fair to say that we sometimes wish we were younger and could turn back the clock. In looking back it is easy to say to ourselves that we could have done so much more and could have done things much different. But at that particular moment in time, it seemed the right option or we may have had no other choice available. How many would agree that we are the perfect age? Would we prefer instead to roll back the years? God always encourages us to do what we can, with what we have and to do it to the best of our ability. Wouldn't it be great if we could say, whatever our age, that we're happy with our lot. We may not be able to roll back the years, but we can ask God's help in making the most of today and every day.

 Notes

Top Speed: These greyhounds churn up the sand on the final straight at Curraheen Park, Bishopstown, Cork

OCTOBER 29TH

'Sometimes people describe their frustration and discouragement in terms of being trapped in closed circuits with no escape. We often speak of going round in circles.' ~*Conor Cunningham*

The experience of going around in circles is universal. Life can become predictable and routine for many people. We like routine. We have to make a deliberate effort to do something different outside of routine. Perhaps we're going around in circles because we feel there's nothing left. We may be feeling guilty, lonely, hurt, misled, misunderstood and upset by something we have done or by something done to us. God has a completely different viewpoint to ours. The invitation always is to step outside any closed circle and to begin to walk the journey of life again. God always wants to shower us with blessings, including peace, love, reassurance, guidance and enthusiasm. These blessings are extended to us within any closed circle but take much more effect when we are willing to step out of that circle and begin to live again.

 Notes

Silhouetted: Tall reeds of grass are silhouetted in evening sunlight over the River Blackwater

OCTOBER 30TH

'Be not like the one who sits by the fireside and watches the fire go out, then blows vainly upon the dead ashes. Do not give up hope or yield to despair because of that which is past, for to bewail the irretrievable is the worst of human frailites.' ~Kahlil Gabran

We all know the comforts of an open fire, especially since the clocks have gone back an hour. Central heating is convenient but will never have the character or warmth of an open fire. But once a fire goes out there is no going back. Ashes can never go back to the warmth and heat they gave out earlier. They have served their purpose and it's time to move on. The same goes with mistakes made or regrets over something in our past. Nothing can undo or change what's happened. If we continue looking into the dead ashes we are stuck. For any healing or growth to take place we must move on or at least take a step forward in hope. In our Gospel stories, Jesus constantly found people looking into dead ashes. He encouraged and gave them permission to move on with their lives. We all need the same from time to time.

 Notes

Pumpkin power: Getting ready for Halloween

OCTOBER 31ST

'Halloween is huge in my house and we really get into the "spirit" of things!' ~*Dee Snider*

Halloween has its origins going right back to our Celtic ancestors who celebrated the feast of Samhain on Nov 1st. They celebrated the new year on this day because it was a time of transition from light to darkness. They also believed that the boundary between the living world and that of the dead was very thin, so much so that the spirits of the dead returned. Some say Halloween is silly nonsense, a commercial opportunity and a waste of money. But Halloween has a lot to offer. Children love it and always will. For adults it brings back childhood memories of snap apple and other simple games that still survive. It puts us in touch with the mystery of life and that some things in life are often clouded in darkness. It put us in touch with the struggle between light and darkness and the struggle between good and evil. Halloween may have pagan origins but the Christian message is wrapped around it. It's a simple Halloween message that God calms, encourages and reassures us, especially when we struggle with darkness, evil, mystery and the unknown.

 Notes

NOVEMBER

Celebration Of Light And Love: Traditionally the lighting of candles is symbolic of prayer, hope and marking something special. Today, All Saints Day, is one of those day.

NOVEMBER 1ST

'I was in love with loving.' – St.Augustine

The following has been written about love. They say it is patient and kind. It sees beyond another's faults, for love, they say, is blind. Love will not diminish or rust or fade with years. But it will gain its strength from time, from laughter, joy and tears. Love is God's own gift to us and a present from above. God gives us peace and God gives us joy. But first of all God gives us love. Today is the Feast of All Saints. At its heart is love. It is a feast day that's all about the love of all our loved ones who have died. These people lived good, decent and down-to-earth lives. They may not have been famous, they may not have made headlines, but in God's eyes they are now celebrities. Today we call them saints and we thank them for all the love they have shown us down through the years.

 Notes

May They Rest In Peace: A photo of St.Mary's Cemetery Millstreet, reminding us to say a prayer for all our loved ones who have died

NOVEMBER 2ND

'We draw encouragement and inspiration from our loved ones who have gone before us and blazed a trail for us. Each one has made the path that bit easier for us.' ~Flor McCarthy

Languages can differ considerably. French as a language will often use two words where English just has the one. An example is 'goodbye'. We just have the one word while the French use 'Au revoir'. Today we celebrate the Feast of All Souls. It is a day when we pause, remember and pray for all our loved ones who have died. Some we got to say goodbye to, while others left us before any goodbyes could be said. Our prayers are an attempt at saying we haven't forgotten them and that they will always be a special part of our lives. The French have another word for goodbyes. They use 'Adieu' reserved for final definitive departures. The nearest English translation is 'until we meet in Heaven'. May all our loved ones who have died rest in peace.

 Notes

Inviting Walkway: A winding path winds its way through Macroom Park, Co.Cork

NOVEMBER 3RD

'God's presence is throughout all creation. When the sun rises in the morning, its rays touch everything in creation at the exact same instant. If God's mind is like the sun's rays, then God knows all the intimate details of all our lives in a single instant.' ~Joseph Girzone

We know how early it gets dark now in the evenings. It's not that the sun stops shining, it's simply that the earth tilts away from the sun a little bit each day creating less light as we head towards the winter solstice. The image of God as light of the world and our lives is comforting. God never abandons any of us even in the midst of our deepest darkness. Every bit of light needs to be harnessed. We do so with a kind word of support, a word of encouragement, a smile, gentle reassurance, a word of thanks, a word of appreciation, a prayer or a smile. All of these and much more remind us of God's gentle presence among us.

 Notes

Artistic Smiles: Niamh O'Neill art teacher in Coláiste Choilm is all smiles next to one of her paintings from the English Market Paintings Exhibition

NOVEMBER 4TH

'It is with the smallest brushes that the artist paints the most exquisitely beautiful pictures'
~Andre Bessette

We all have our own favourite painting hanging up at home. We may have got it as a gift but the chances are high that you bought it and you did so because it caught your eye and imagination. Lots of brushes are used to create each painting but it's the smallest ones that bring out the finer details. The same goes with all we do in life. Big sweeping changes and happenings in life are rare. But God always calls us to work with the smallest of brushes. Even if we don't do it, God most certainly does. We are the canvas, God is the artist. But for the artist to work, the canvas must be open, welcome and receptive. It's with all the small bits and pieces put together that God creates something special. That something special is you.

 Notes

Reflective Waters: One of the lakes at Glendalough, Co. Wicklow, reflects a beautiful winter skyline

NOVEMBER 5TH

It's All In What You Say…

Image today seems to be everything. Huge amounts of money are spent on advertising telling us what to buy, what to wear, how to stay young and healthy. Appearance seems to be what we are really concerned about. There is a fear of growing old and instead an obsession with staying young forever. It is of course good to be concerned with physical appearance, on being healthy and feeling good about ourselves. But there is not enough attention on looking after the soul or spirit of each person and we have all neglected the sacred within. We carry around too many burdens, hurts, worries and scars within us. We don't give ourselves a chance to let some of them go and instead we don't give a fair chance to nurture all the goodness and reservoirs of love within each of us. In our Gospels Jesus sought to bring balance to every person, not just on the outside but also within. Today we are experts in what to wear, what to eat, how to exercise-but not in balance. Unless we go the step further and nurture our soul or spirit we will always be out of balance.

 Notes

Day 310

Cheeky Robin: A friendly robin watches proceedings in the restaurant at Griffin's Gardening Centre, Dripsey, Co.Cork

NOVEMBER 6TH

'Years wrinkle the skin but to give up enthusiasm wrinkles the soul. ~Douglas MacArthur

It is hard to be enthusiastic during the month of November. Many find this month long and dreary. With darkness falling earlier each evening it's not easy to be upbeat all the time. The word enthusiasm comes from the ancient Greek word "En" + "Theos", meaning 'inspired by God'. So a great starting place is to pray to God for some inspiration. We're not looking for a fireworks display but for an ability to be enthusiastic about the many little things and jobs we do each day. These make up a fine collection of which we can be very proud of. We sometimes wait for something big to happen when in fact it is often happening quietly all around us.

 Notes

Beauty Beyond The Branches: A pheasant with striking colours is partially hidden at the Mardyke, Cork

NOVEMBER 7TH

How good are you at maths?...........

Think of a number. It does not matter what the number is so long as you can think of it and not forget it. Now multiply it by two. Add ten. Now divide that number by two. Now this is the last bit, with the number you have subtract the number you first chose. Your answer will be five. No matter what number you choose the answer will always be five. It's not magic, just one of those formulas that will always pull in the same answer no matter what you begin with. If five is the common link in this formula, then the one word that would sum up the five in all of our lives is love. Everyone has it in some shape or form. Without it we cannot survive. Without it we are cold, indifferent, cruel, hostile and unforgiving. Jesus in our Gospels did his best to nurture and highlight the number five in everyone's life. No matter what our situation or no matter what is going on for us everything points back to love. Try any number or combination above and you will always come back to five!

 Notes

Hanging On: A Goldfinch rests a moment for his lunch

NOVEMBER 8TH

'I fear waking up one morning and finding out my life was all for nothing. We're here for a reason. I believe a bit of the reason is to throw little torches out to lead people through the dark.'
~Whoopie Goldberg

What a pity if it dawned on us, that our life was all for nothing and a waste of time. That must surely be the one of the saddest moments in life that we could face. But life can slip by so quickly. The pace of life is hectic, full and competitive. We are at times almost forced to keep up with it. Then one day we look in the mirror, we see uncertainty in our lives, we begin to question what we have achieved and we feel that everything has slipped us by. But that day can be firmly kept at a distance if we treasure each day as a gift from God to us and if we treasure the small moments that always add up to something significant. It can be kept at a distance if we share some of our light with others whose light is dim or struggling. Our day will come too when we will need someone else to help ours. What can I do today that will add to my sense of purpose in life? Whatever small good I may do today will have an impact way beyond my limited horizons.

 Notes

Jar Of Blessings: A jar of blessings on display in the prayer room at Grace Dieu Retreat House, near Tramore, Co. Waterford

NOVEMBER 9TH

'Goodness is the only investment that never fails.' —Henry David Thoreau

A young boy was promised an ice cream cone if he was good while accompanying his grandfather on some errands. The longer they were gone the more difficult the boy was finding it to be good. "How much longer will it be?" he asked. "Not too long," replied the grandfather, "We've just one more stop." The young boy replied "I don't know if I can make it grandad, I can be good. I just can't be good enough, long enough!!" It is always a challenge to be good and to keep doing what we think is best. Formally this is called 'a moral conscience'. But God puts it much more simply, 'Do to others what you would like them to do to you.'

 Notes

'Hitching A Ride' It's a perfect balancing act in the NEC Killarney, but how many riders can you see on this bike?!!

NOVEMBER 10TH

'De mortuis nil nisi bonum' ~Old Latin Phrase

The above phrase translates as 'say nothing but good about those who have died.' The same phrase goes back many hundreds of years but is full of wisdom and insight. As we continue to remember those who have died during this month of November, we are encouraged to think only of their goodness and love. Is this not hypocritical? Not so. If we are made in the image of God then God's goodness can be seen in every human person. By concentrating on their goodness we are in someway connecting with God's love and goodness. It also gives us encouragement too. We can see what we ourselves might or could be doing. Remembering and praying for our loved ones who have died can be sad and lonely but it can also give us encouragement to keep going, and especially when we miss them the most.

 Notes

Intimate Moment: Jodi Cronin and Aiden Fitzgerald share an intimate moment at Waterloo, near Blarney, Co.Cork

NOVEMBER 11TH

'When people forget what you said, they will remember you were there with them.' ~Robin Eeames

There are often occasions when we simply don't know what to say. Words seem inappropriate and almost out of place. Sympathising with someone who has lost a loved one through death is a good example. Robin Eames recalled how he met families after the Omagh bombing and he remembers the utter and complete silence. He quietly prayed 'God, tell me what to say.' He then recalled how his greatest gift that day was to simply be with the families and to embrace the silence. When we journey with anyone, the greatest gift we can give is to simply be there for them and with them. It's not about words but much more about a gentle presence. It is a most precious gift that becomes even more precious with time.

 Notes

Mirror Reflections: Cork City Hall is reflected with great beauty across the River Lee

NOVEMBER 12TH

Carl Jung was a world-famous psychologist who studied human behaviour at great length and shared many thoughts on why people do certain things.

Many people made appointments to see him. One day a wealthy lady phoned him to request an urgent appointment the next day at 3 pm. He said it wouldn't be possible because he was committed to an important appointment at that time. The following day the same lady happened to be in a boat sailing past his garden which led down to the shore of the Lake of Zurich. There she could see him, sitting on a low wall with his shoes and socks off, dangling his feet in the water. She was angry that he had lied to her and that he had no appointment at all. She arrived home and rang him straight away: "You said you couldn't see me because you had a very important engagement. But I just saw you now doing nothing and sitting on the shore of the lake by yourself." He replied: "I told you no lie. I had an appointment. It has been the most important appointment of the week, an appointment with myself." Have I made an appointment with myself today or indeed for the coming week?

 Notes

Inside Out!: Students from Coláiste Choilm trying to come to grips with the weather conditions at Ross Castle, Killarney

NOVEMBER 13TH

Lord, help me never judge someone before I know the score. Not until I've walked in someone's shoes a mile or more. Let me be quick to understand and slow to criticise. The world is a very different place viewed through another's eye. So help me Lord, to show understanding and care, as the one who will always be ready to walk another mile with those who ask of me. ~Old Prayer

Some of our old prayers are full of wisdom. This one is honest and full of gentle advice. So often we are quick to condemn and judge. We assume we know the whole story which gives us the right to say what we want. But we don't know the whole story, and certainly not until we walk in another person's shoes. That doesn't just happen. It means hearing and listening, with openness and honesty. It means giving someone a complete chance to say everything without condemnation.

 Notes

Steeple Views: These brave lumberjacks working at great heights up on St. Finbarr's Cathedral, Cork

NOVEMBER 14TH

The following reflection was read during a prayer service at Coláiste Choilm called 'God doesn't ask'.........

God doesn't ask if you are an honours or pass candidate but asks how you treat the people you meet each day. God doesn't ask who designed your clothes but asks how many people we care for each day. God doesn't ask how much money you have but asks if you earned it honestly and spent it wisely. God doesn't ask what result you got in your last exam but asks if you performed to the best of your ability. God doesn't ask how many friends you have but asks how many people you have been a friend to. God doesn't ask what your address is but asks how you treat your neighbours. God doesn't ask about the colour of your skin but asks about the content of your character. God doesn't ask how many awards you have won but asks how many people you helped. God doesn't ask how many hours you prayed but asks how genuine your prayers are. God doesn't ask what you do in life but asks how you live your life.

 Notes

Surf Time: Picturesque Garretstown Beach which is hugely popular for surfers of all ages and experience

NOVEMBER 15TH

'Every day, another person dies or is seriously injured on our roads. This can't go on. We remember those who have died, we think of the never-ending grief of their loved ones and then we think about how we can change our own behaviour to ensure that we and our family are safe on the road.'
~Gay Byrne

World Remembrance Day for road traffic victims is marked each year during the middle of November. It is a day to remember those whose lives have been tragically lost on our roads and whose families have been devastated. Speed causes 40% of all fatal crashes each year. At 100kmp (60mph) we travel 88 feet in just one second. The faster we go the greater the distance we will need to stop. If only we could slow down a little. If only there was no drink driving. If only everyone wore their seat belt. In Ireland at least, attitudes are changing slowly but we have a long way to go. We all have a part to play in road safety. But today we pause and pray for all those who have died from a road traffic accident. We especially remember their families.

 Notes

Soaring: A sea bird soars with the wind under the cliffs at Wicklow Head

NOVEMBER 16TH

'Private prayer is habit-forming, make it part of your life and you will not want to live without it anytime soon. But it would be a mistake to think that it exhausts the possibilities of living the spiritual life. Besides praying by yourself, there is much, much more.' – *Barbara Cawthorne Crafton*

It is good to take a moment for our own quiet prayer. It is quality time out that no one can take away from us, a moment when we can simply be ourselves. It allows us to be honest and express whatever is going on for us. But it is also good to pray as part of a community. Praying with others gives us the sense of a journey together and that we are not in isolation. Praying together allows us to support and encourage each other. Most of the major religions in the world actively encourage community participation. It is all about finding the balance between what is private and what we do together. Personal prayer gives so many comfort and a sense of purpose. But it can never be done exclusively on our own.

 Notes

Winter Landscape: A row of trees are reflected on the water near Macroom, Co.Cork

NOVEMBER 17TH

'Hassled families need to hear this message, that rising to attend to a child at 3 o'clock in the morning is holy and is a prayer, that breastfeeding is a prayer, that making time to listen and explain is a prayer, that teaching children to ride a bike is prayer, that training them to do chores at home is a prayer and that playing football in the garden is a prayer.' ~Michael Quinn

Parents have initial difficulties in accepting that many of the things they do at home are deeply spiritual. How does one believe that ironing clothes, changing nappies, making lunches, playing cards or making love has anything to do with God? The answer is simple, when any act is done in love and out of love we can be certain that God is there too. This should be inspiring and liberating. Formal religious practice in the past often put blinkers on people's eyes in their search for God. This has changed considerably today and the blinkers are down but maybe they need to come down more. God's presence can be found where ever love is. These many miracles of love are often to be found at home. There is a lot of prayer going on quietly and without fuss each day. It would be a pity to take it for granted.

 Notes

Moving Up River: A swan glides along the River Lee near the Mercy Hospital, Cork

NOVEMBER 18TH

A reflection called 'Stop Supposing' ~ The Author is unknown

Don't start your day by supposing that trouble is just ahead. It's better to stop supposing and start with a prayer instead. For what is the use of supposing the dire things that could happen to you. Why worry about some misfortune that seldom, if ever, comes true. But instead of just idle supposing, why not step forward to meet each new day secure in the knowledge that God is near you to lead you each step of the way. For supposing the worst things will happen only helps to make them come true. So if you desire to be happy just give up supposing the worst things and look for the best things instead.

 Notes

Stretching Towards The Light: A red leaf glistens as it soaks up sunlight

NOVEMBER 19TH

'Sometimes it may be an illness that becomes our new teacher or bereavement or the birth of a child or falling in love. Anything that shakes us out of our slumber and opens us to wider and deeper experience is a spiritual friend worthy of our gratitude.' ~Donagh O'Shea

It is easy to be complacent and take much for granted all around us. Every day presents us with new challenges and opportunities. We do our best to make the most of them as they come. But some days can be hugely challenging to the point where it's a struggle to cope. We might not see such days as a friend. It is even tempting to push them to one side in the hope that tomorrow will be better. It is tempting to blame those around us, particularly our nearest and dearest. It is even tempting to blame ourselves. Spiritual wisdom encourages us to hold these days because we learn and grow from them. This is different to wailing and moaning in self pity. When we hit difficult and tough days we move deeper and we ask God for the strength, courage and hope to rise above them.

 Notes

The Great Flood: What a difference a few days can make. Both photos were taken in the same spot but it can be seen how the weir at Ballincollig Regional Park ceased to be during the great flood

NOVEMBER 20TH

'In Asia they say that life is a great river and it will flow, no matter what you do or don't do. We can decide to flow with the river or to battle it. The river doesn't care. Life doesn't care.' ~Vincent Travers

So much can be said about rivers. We are only too aware of the great power of a river in flood and in contrast the beauty of a gentle flowing river in the height of summer. Every river has an energy and flow that nothing can stop. Even a dam has its limits. Comparing life to a river is a good image. The many meandering twists and turns of a river reflect life and its unpredictability. Every day brings us some measure of how uncertain life can be. Life can be so uplifting and rewarding but just as quick it can be cruel and unforgiving. We have no option but to go with the flow. Where does God come into the whole picture? I like the image of the banks on either side of the river that somehow guide the flow of the river. God is there to guide us along through the unpredictable nature of life. It may seem sometimes that God is not around because rivers do flood but even in a flood the banks on either side are still doing a job.

 Notes

Obstacle Course: A SUV grinds to a halt in front of a fallen tree at Tooreenbawn, Millstreet

NOVEMBER 21ST

The Paradox Of Our Age...

The paradox of our age in history is that we have taller buildings but shorter tempers. We have wider roads but narrower viewpoints. We spend more but have less and we buy more but enjoy it less. We have bigger houses and more conveniences, but less time. We have more experts but more problems, more medicine but less well-being. We have multiplied our possessions but reduced our values. We've learned to make a living but not a life. We've added years to life, not life to years. We've been all the way to the moon and back but have trouble crossing the street to meet a new neighbour. We've conquered outer space but not inner space. We've done larger things but not better things. We've cleaned up the air but polluted the soul, split the atom but not our prejudice. We plan more but accomplish less. We've learned to rush but not to wait. We've become long on quantity but short on quality. But there is time when we can choose either to make a difference or do nothing at all.

 Notes

Cosy Log Fire: There is nothing quite like a cosy log fire during these days of winter

NOVEMBER 22ND

'To stop the flow of music would be like the stopping of time itself, incredible and inconceivable.'
~Aaron Copland

Today is the Feast of St.Cecilia. She is the patroness of music and musicians. We so often take music for granted and yet it is the pulse and heartbeat of life. Music is there for every occasion. It can uplift and it can calm and relax. It can unite and break down barriers. It has been said that music and silence combine strongly because music is done with silence and silence is full of music. We live in a noisy world with little room for quiet time and silence. Quiet, relaxing music can lead us to a much quieter place where we can often encounter the gentle quiet presence of God. Today we thank God and Cecilia for the great gift of music. As the old saying puts it so well: 'When words fail, music speaks.'

 Notes

Chimney Views: A disused chimney tower is silhouetted against a colourful November sunset near Glanmire, Co.Cork

NOVEMBER 23RD

'Some people believe too strongly. Of course religious leaders will say the opposite, that faith can never be too strong. Maybe just a dot of belief would save the secularist from absorption into their culture and a dot of unbelief might save the devotee from drowning in their faith.' ~Thomas Moore

Striking the balance in what we do is a life-long task and more so when it comes to matters of belief. It has been well documented the many benefits of believing in God, but some people believe too strongly. Pure belief leaves little room for movement and openness. There is no room for reflection, no freedom to question and there is a sense of having it all worked out. But no one can surely have it all worked out in a world more infinitely complex than our own beliefs. A small amount of unbelief is normal, important and is an honest recognition that we live in a complex world. That is why St.Thomas is such an important figure in our Gospel stories. He doubted, he questioned and most importantly he went on to become an inspiration to so many.

 Notes

Flying Stones: A rally car puts stones flying near Clonakilty, west Cork

NOVEMBER 24TH

'The wind blows where it chooses but you do not know where it comes from or where it goes. So it is with everyone who is born of the Spirit.' ~John 3:8

There is a lovely story told about an eight-year-old boy called Sam who asked a very honest question: "What if everybody in the whole world laughed at the same time? What would it sound like?" No doubt he thought it would make a big difference. 'What if' questions are always full of possibility and potential. 'What if' questions have led to many new discoveries, particularly in the area of medicine. The same can happen in the area of spirituality. What if we all were open to the spirit of God in our lives? What if we all did something good and positive together instead of moan and complain? What if we all said a prayer for someone in need today or for a special intention? Why not make a 'what if' happen today?

 Notes

Rambo: A ram poses for a quick snap

NOVEMBER 25TH

'When are you too old? Only on the day when you truly have nothing left to give. And the good news is this, that day never has to arrive' ~Author Unknown

Old age has officially been described as nearing or surpassing the average life span of human beings and thus the end of the human life cycle. During the month of November we get in touch much more with the inevitability of human life ending. It's something we're not too comfortable with. Yet it's something we all have to face. Older people are much more in touch with the cycles of life. They have been through life's many experiences, have seen much and are aware of how fragile life is from the cradle to the grave. They have much to teach us and we have much to learn from them. In particular we can learn from their ability to continue to give and to contribute to life in so many different ways. What they have given and continue to give is a gentle reminder to us to be open to one of God's precious gifts, the gift of today.

 Notes

'November Smiles' Matthew O'Sullivan and Hollie Walker are all smiles as they go on stage to perform 'Hairspray' at Coláiste Choilm, Ballincollig

NOVEMBER 26TH

'So who are the needy? I am. You are. Everyone is. Today, I may help you but tomorrow I may need you to help me.' – The Universe

One of the biggest negatives to be found in society today is how the individual is forgotten. Surely we are more than just a number or a statistic or a face in the crowd. We have lost the ability to connect with one person. To lose that is to lose something great and precious. We all have needs and concerns. No one person has it all worked out. No one person is fully safe or secure. No one is shielded from the knocks of life. Our greatest privilege is to connect with someone in our lives today. No matter how small that connection may be, it is uniquely precious. The chance may never come again. When we continue making many connections, great things begin to happen. God is always the link in each of these connections.

 Notes

Winter Skyline: Even in the depths of winter nature can still work God's paintbrush with style!

NOVEMBER 27TH

'If you reach for a goal, you may not get there, but at least you'll get a lot further than if you hadn't reached at all.' ~ Author Unknown

It is good to have goals. Some are long-term, some short-term and many of them are about today. All the bits and pieces of today make up our own unique story. Each story is special and important but also each of our stories is complex and varied. We deal with each day as it comes and unfolds. It is God's gift to us to use in the best way we can. To have a goal each day is always good and important. It is good to be motivated, to have a sense of purpose and to know that all will be well. It's not about getting everything we do right, it's not about trying to get everything done but all about giving each day our best attempt. We can do absolutely nothing more than that. Even if things don't work out, at least we will have made so much more progress than by doing nothing at all.

 Notes

Night Time In Macroom: A night view looking across at the castle grounds from Masseytown

NOVEMBER 28TH

'Consult not your fears but your hopes and your dreams. Think not about your frustrations but about your unfulfilled potential. Concern yourself not with what you tried and failed in, but with what it is still possible for you to do.' – *Pope John 23rd*

It is so easy to focus in on our limitations, fears and what we can't do. If we keep hearing it all around us, it is easy for us to begin to believe it. Many lack self confidence and an inner belief that 'much is possible'. Our Gospel stories make no apologies about encouraging us to concentrate on our hopes, dreams, potential, spiritual growth and our ability to seize endless possibilities all around us. These stories acknowledge our own difficulties and struggles but they never glorify or sensationalise negative news. Maybe during the coming week could be a good time to start focusing not on everything that's negative, useless and unfulfilling but instead begin celebrating our hopes, dreams, potential and everything that we are so good at doing.

 Notes

Smile!!: A farmer has a sense of humour with these silage bales, in an attempt to keep the crows at bay

NOVEMBER 29TH

God's Voice…

It is the voice of reaching out, courage, healing and forgiveness. In the hospital ward it's the voice of a friendly word or a gentle prayer. In the home it's the voice of love, companionship and togetherness. In the school it's the voice of laughter and shouting in the playground. In nature it's the voice of a gentle breeze, the sound of birds singing, raindrops, running streams or the waves lapping on the sea shore. In a church it's the voice of a community praying to their God. If we pause for a brief moment, no matter where we might be or the time of the day, God's voice is all around us, loud and clear. Often it's the voice of God full of surprises. We will find that God's voice is all around us but to hear it we must listen carefully!

 Notes

Maximising The Wind: These kitesurfers are busy maximising the wind at Lahinch looking across at Liscannor on Hag's Head, Co.Clare

NOVEMBER 30TH

'Once the chess game is over, the king and pawn go back into the same box.' ~Italian Proverb

Sometimes it's hard for us to understand that in God's eyes we are all equal and the same, with no exception. We are of course different in terms of gifts, talents, personality, fingerprint, DNA and so on. To put it simply, God has no favourites. It is we who make the distinctions in life. It is we who categorise people and put them where we want them put. Some people seem to be successful while others simply struggle to keep up with the pace of life. Many get left behind. Yet every person has a right to be recognised as an equal, to feel important and loved and to feel that they have an important contribution to make in life. Am I a king or a pawn? Am I inclusive of others? Do I cherish the contribution of others, particularly someone who may have low self esteem or someone who feels left behind in life?

 Notes

DECEMBER

Crash And Splash: The power of the sea is always eye-catching on the Dingle Peninsula, West Kerry

DECEMBER 1ST

'Simplicity asks us to sit and listen to those other whispers inside us that we seldom have time to hear. It helps us to discover the happiness that comes, not from having an abundance of money and things but from having space for intimacy in our friendships, space for ourselves and primarily space for God.' ~Ruth Valerio

These early days of December are marked by the beginning of our journey through Advent. It's not a word that you will find in many shopping catalogues. Few will get excited about Advent and yet it is a season full of meaning and symbolism. The word "Advent" is derived from the Latin "Adventus", a name which means coming or arrival. The prayers of Advent touch on each person walking in some darkness and yet awaiting and anticipating a great light. It is a time for us to hear those other quiet whispers in our lives of a God gently calling us from darkness into light. Advent is a reminder of how we need this light more than ever in our own lives.

 Notes

At Top Speed: An enthusiastic dog runs along Tramore beach, Co.Waterford

DECEMBER 2ND

'Anger is a normal human emotion, created by God and given to us as a gift.' ~*Fran Ferder*

Not everyone can see anger as a gift and for that matter to see it as a gift from God. The emphasis has always been on the negative when it comes to anger. We have been told that anger is wrong, that it is to be avoided and to offer it up. Such an emphasis has glaring potential problems. Not dealing with anger means it becomes repressed. Anything repressed will always re-emerge in some way. Repressed anger can lead to depression and other related illnesses. Flying off the handle in an outburst of anger or rage is also not the way to go. The challenge is to understand, accept and integrate our anger and to learn to use it for good. Jesus in our Gospels did just that. He did not repress or hide his feelings. He encouraged others to do the same helping them to become mature, balanced and ready to face all of life's eventualities.

 Notes

'In Love' Two calves getting intimate at Kilmorna Heights, Ballyvolane, Cork

DECEMBER 3RD

'From small beginnings come great things.' ~Proverb quote

The huge Melrose Suspension Bridge spans the Niagara River and links Canada and the United States. They say that the bridge was built in the following way. First a kite was flown across the river. Attached to the kite was a piece of string. Attached to this piece of string was a rope and onto the rope was attached a steel cable. The steel cable was then used to get the rest of the bridge in place. The story of the Melrose bridge illustrates how great things often have humble beginnings. Whatever our expectations are for this month we must always hold the piece of string. If we can do that it means we are in control. When it comes to faith matters the pieces of string are even more important. If we don't hold the string then it can never become a rope, a steel cable and so on. Maybe we think our piece of string is insignificant. In God's eyes it is hugely significant and for this month of December the invitation is to treasure all the many little contributions we bring to each day.

 Notes

Yes It's Me!: Ciara O'Flynn enjoys a lighter moment of a photo taken of herself on display at a photography exhibition by Padraig Spillane

DECEMBER 4TH

A prayer for December…

We give you praise, O God, for everything that is new and beautiful, for everything which holds promise and brings us joy throughout this month of December. Help us to make the most of every chance we have to start afresh. May we show love to one another and to all. Help us to forgive others as we receive your forgiveness. Help us to listen when we should and to find the best words when we speak. We thank you for our friends. Help us to be good friends to those closest and dearest to us. Help us to be patient with ourselves and with others. Keep us safe each day. Be with us as we travel each day. Help us to be aware of your love shown to us in the people around us. Bless all those who need our help and particularly anyone who is feeling sad or down at this time. Help us to live as well as we can, giving thanks and glory to you, O God. Amen.

 Notes

Colour Fish: A trip to Ocean World in Dingle is always a treat with so many colourful fish to be seen

DECEMBER 5TH

'God does not ask you to be a monk or a hermit. You must be silent in the way God asks you to be silent.'
~Vincent Pallotti

Sometimes the thought of complete silence, quietness and time on our own is most appealing. The life of a hermit may seem attractive during these few weeks before Christmas but the reality is that few of us would last even a day! We have grown so accustomed to noise in our daily lives that silence is something that's difficult for most. Yet silence is a precious gift that needs to be experienced little and often. A common link in all of the great spiritual writers is to find that space in our lives which we can claim as our own. Advent is all about trying to find such a space and when we find it, even if it's only for a few moments, we can be sure that we are indeed close to God.

 Notes

Here Comes Santa: Santa makes a perfect touchdown at Blarney, Co.Cork

DECEMBER 6TH

'Yes, there is a Santa Claus. He exists as certainly as love, generosity and devotion exist. How dreary our world if there were no Santa Claus. The eternal light with which childhood fills the world would be extinguished.' ~Francis Church

Today is the feast of St.Nicholas. He came from a wealthy family and decided to give all his money to the poor. He always did so quietly and without fuss. He would drop some gold coins down the chimney of those who were really poor. People wondered who the generous donor was. One day someone found out it was Nicholas. His name and fame began to spread to many countries and so Santa Claus as we know him today came into being. We give gifts at Christmas because we know deep within that it's good to express our love for those who are special and important to us. Thanks to Nicholas, Santa is alive and well. Our world would be such a darker place without his inspiring presence.

 Notes

One Step At A Time!: A swan carefully makes its way across The Lough in Cork after it froze over

DECEMBER 7TH

"Have patience with all things, but chiefly have patience with yourself." ~St.Francis de Sales

There is a lovely Jewish story from ancient times about an old man who was in his hundredth year and who wandered into Abraham's camp just before nightfall. Abraham welcomed the man and offered him hospitality. While the food was cooking Abraham suggested that they pray together. Abraham raised his hands and his eyes towards heaven and began the evening prayer. After a while he saw the old man worshipping the camp fire. Stopping for a moment he corrected the old man and asked him to direct his prayers to the Almighty. But the old man went back worshipping the fire. This went on a few times and Abraham lost his patience and kicked the old man out of the camp. He went back to prayer "See Lord, how much I love you." There was silence and then he heard the Lord say, "Abraham, I have put up with that old man and his unusual ways for the past 100 years and you cannot put up with him even for five minutes!"

 Notes

'Advent Light' A candle sets off lovely light in St.Patrick's Church, Millstreet

DECEMBER 8TH

Mary is not alive in statues and pictures but in the real and powerful change that can be brought in the world when God's preferences and God's choices are taken seriously.' —Denis McBride

Today is the Feast of the Immaculate Conception and it is a recognition of Mary's lack of flaws and weaknesses. In fact she had none. Surely this feast is a putdown? How can we live up to Mary? Where do we even begin? The purpose of today's feast day is to mark Mary out as someone special as the mother of Jesus but it doesn't mark her out as removed or distant from us. Like us, she experienced the fragility of life and experienced many unexpected and difficult moments in her life. But at all times she put her trust in God. This is the challenge for us. Where would the world be if everyone just thought of themselves independent of others and of God? Today's feast day traditionally marks the countdown to Christmas but it's also a day to ask Mary's many blessings on each of us.

 Notes

December Frost: A clump of frozen grass sparkles in early morning sunshine

DECEMBER 9TH

'Advent is a reminder of the importance of growth. It reminds me of the last month of a pregnancy, when you are aching and weary and just longing for birth, but the child will only come in his or her own sweet time.' –Breda O'Brien

Each of us stands at the fork of a road in life. This season of Advent coming into Christmas is no exception. I can travel the Advent road or as some people call it, 'the road less travelled'. Or I can travel the main road to Christmas, the dual carriageway of busyness, rushing here and there, deadlines, parties, running out of time, to the point of exhaustion. The Advent road invites us to take a closer look at our lives, to see what areas we could change. It also encourages us to look at areas where growth could take place. The Advent road is making time to prioritise what is essential and important in my life. All main roads are attractive and important but the Advent road, even if it is less travelled, gives us many options.

 Notes

Flooded Gateway: A gate is nearly covered in floodwater at Mallow Co.Cork

DECEMBER 10TH

'To be good instruments of God's love we must avoid being over-tired, burnt-out, stressed, aggressive, dispersed or closed-up. We need to be rested, centred, peaceful and aware of the needs of our body, our heart and our spirit.' ~Jean Vanier

When we are tired it is hard to do anything. It is even more difficult on a spiritual level, to do anything proper. The invitation each day is to share God's love with other people, but only if we ourselves are relaxed and rested. It is always a difficult challenge to find the balance between work, rest and play. As we journey through this month of December it might seem wishful thinking to be rested and peaceful. But no one else is going to do it for us and no one is going to thank us if we don't.

 Notes

Cute And Cuddly: These polar bears add a lovely Christmas touch at Griffin's Gardening Centre, Dripsey

DECEMBER 11TH

A little story…

There's a story told about a hare who was incredibly fast and who was always teasing a tortoise who was very slow. "I wouldn't be surprised if you were the slowest creature in the world," teased the hare. "Oh, I think I could move fast enough if I had to," said the tortoise, inching his way along. The hare pushed the tortoise to a race. The hare set off at a great pace and soon left the tortoise far behind. Before long the winning post was upon him. Suddenly an idea came to him as he skidded to a halt. "I'll really rub it in and wait until the tortoise is nearly at the line. Then I'll fly past him." With that the hare sat under a tree and waited but being a hot day fell fast asleep. Meanwhile the slow old tortoise had been plodding along. He eventually passed the sleeping hare and the winning post. The cheers woke the hare but it was too late.

The moral of the story: Slow and steady can win the race of life.

 Notes

Moon Eclipse: A partial eclipse of the moon

DECEMBER 12TH

A morning prayer.......

Thank you O Lord, for loving me. You are with me always. I thank you for the gift of being alive this morning. I thank you for the sleep which has refreshed me. I thank you for the chance to begin life all over again. Lord, this day is full of promise and opportunity. Help me to waste none of it. This day is full of mystery and the unknown. Help me to face it without fear or anxiety. Help me to be fully alive to it all. During this day may I become a more thoughtful person, a more prayerful person, a more generous and kindly person. Help me not to be turned in on myself but to be sensitive and helpful to others. Let me do nothing today that will hurt anyone, but if I do, help me to get back on track again. I ask you to bless me throughout this day in all I hope to do. Later on when evening and night comes, may I look back on this day without regrets. May I be grateful for all my blessings. I make this prayer in your name. Amen

 Notes

Mirror Views: Some beautiful scenery from Co.Mayo seen from a different angle

DECEMBER 13TH

'In healing one can concentrate on either of two attributes, the power of God or the love of God. But in every healing there is a manifestation of both.' ~*Francis MacNutt*

There is a part of everyone's life that needs healing. It isn't just confined to health but it can be any part of our lives that needs the gentle touch of God. Medicine is one of God's gifts to initiate and sustain healing but all the prescriptions in the world cannot compete with deep spiritual healing. If we are not open to healing itself, it will struggle to happen in our lives. Our prayer today as we move closer to Christmas is to pray for God's gentle healing and gentle touch in our lives. We ask for this especially in those areas of our lives that are vulnerable and exposed. We also include those parts of our lives that need closure. With every healing is the promise of new life and new beginnings, especially this Christmas.

 Notes

Chocolate Train: Lydia O'Connor's gets ready for Christmas at Coláiste Choilm with this masterpiece

DECEMBER 14TH

Tell someone there are 300 billion stars in the universe and they will believe you. Tell them a bench has wet paint on it and they will have to touch it to be sure. ~*Murphy's Law*

It is sometimes easier to tell our life story to a stranger than to someone close to us. There is a feeling that a stranger will not question or judge us whereas someone close to us may do so. As we journey through this month of December and closer to Christmas the invitation is to see God, not as a stranger but as someone who is close and near. No matter what our story God always understands and never judges or condemns. Nothing that has happened, is happening or will happen can ever change this. But like wet paint we're always slow to accept this. We need to touch it to be sure whether it's wet or dry. God is indeed close and near to us. Nothing or nobody can take this away from us.

 Notes

Party Girls: Leigh Galvin, Ann McKenna, Sarah Galvin and Linda Fitzgerald enjoying a Christmas night out in town

DECEMBER 15TH

'It's the start that stops most people' ~ Author Unknown

We get through a lot of stuff each day. December is a month when this becomes nearly unmanageable. At a closer look we could let go of some unnecessary stuff that makes up our lot each day. We all have great plans to do different things but an already cluttered schedule means there isn't time. Some of these plans are good in themselves. These plans may include care of ourselves, plans to include quiet time and plans to spend more time with our family. Many of these revolve around what's precious and important. But often there isn't time. So to make these plans possible, what can I knock off my list of unnecessary stuff that is not life giving? There is always something glaringly obvious. We ask God to help us to get in touch with what is important and precious to us this Christmas.

 Notes

A Deer Stare : A stag deer with some very impressive antlers near Ballinagree, Co.Cork

DECEMBER 16TH

Don't walk in front of me, I may not follow. Don't walk behind me, I may not lead. Walk beside me and just be my friend. ~Author Unknown

There are high expectations put on all of us in these days before Christmas. Some of these are artificially high. We're expected to be in good form, to be in good spirits, to be able to buy gifts at ease and to be in many places at one time. Not everyone can meet these high expectations. This can lead to so much unnecessary stress and worry. The greatest gift we can give to those closest to us is to walk with them and be their friend. When we do this we pull down all expectations and allow someone just to be themselves. No shopping catalogue could ever match such a gift.

 Notes

Limited Light: As we approach the Winter Solstice, a sunset on the hills reminding us that light can still make a decisive impression in the midst of darkness

DECEMBER 17TH

'We need to show that the message of Jesus is indeed good news, not boring or suffocating or restrictive, but extraordinary, life-enhancing and life-changing good news.' ~Gerard Moloney

It is a waste of time complaining about the commercial side of Christmas. Nothing can stop this momentum. Likewise, it's futile giving out about those who do not go to church. Equally futile is pointing the finger of blame. Much more important is to nurture and encourage what is glaringly obvious. The good news of Jesus is indeed extraordinary, life-enhancing and life-changing. But it often gets lost in a lot of unnecessary complaining and wishful thinking. The challenge is to bring this good news alive and to believe that it does make a difference. This is at the heart of the Christmas message. The birth of Jesus is a reminder of God with us and among us. It's not just about some event in the past, but all about the difference it can make in our lives right now.

 Notes

Charity Smiles: Róisín Nic Cárthaigh and Caitríona Ní Chathasaigh from Gaelcholáiste Choilm, Ballincollig, are all smiles as they collect for SHARE at Daunt's Square, Cork

DECEMBER 18TH

'Human systems are imperfect and the hopes they generate are correspondingly fragile. Hope really knows but one true essence: Hope with a capital H – Hope of the eternal kind.' ~John Waters

We are all aware how on occasions our hopes have been built up and then knocked and pulled from us when we least expected it to happen. Life is fragile and our daily activities don't always work out the way we want. Hope is a word that is often spoken about, but it's often built on shallow foundations. Hope is at the core of the Christian message and when we put it in such a context it takes on a new meaning. Very simply 'hope' becomes 'HOPE'. Today and every day towards Christmas we pray to God to instil hope and a sense of purpose and meaning in all we do each day.

 Notes

December Colour: Even in December the staff garden at Coláiste Choilm looks colourful

DECEMBER 19TH

'Be what you is, cuz if you be what you ain't, then you ain't what you is.'
– Tombstone Inscription, Arizona

'Just be yourself' is such apt advice for all of us no matter what our age. It is what Jesus said in different ways to so many people. So often we're trying to be somebody else and it just doesn't work. To be ourself is easier said than done. It means accepting ourselves as we are. We're not perfect but then no-one else is. We can stand with great courage and conviction when we can say we know ourselves, with all our good and not-so-good points. Better again is when we can accept ourselves as we are. Coming up to Christmas there is a subtle pressure to be someone else through clever advertising. The best gift we can give ourselves and others is to be simply be ourselves.

 Notes

Merry Christmas: The family home of the Pecks comes alive with colour and light at Christmas on the outskirts of Ballincollig

DECEMBER 20TH

Another angle on Christmas…

In his book 'Christmas Spoken Here', John Killinger describes how one day he was staring through the window of a beautiful little Christmas shop. It was packed with Christmas items. There were elves, a colourful Santa, sleighs, reindeers, bells, trees and music boxes. There were candles, electric lights, angels, wise men, drummer boys, stars, snowmen and so much more. The little shop was bursting with Christmas. It was infectious. Down in the corner of the front door, where no one could miss it, was the neatest touch of all. It was a small sign that said: "Christmas Spoken Here". In the final run-in to Christmas it could be easy to lose sight of what it's all about. But whenever we speak the "language of Christmas" we are in touch with the heart of it all. It is the language of love, a language that speaks about God who became a little child, born into our world, born into our darkness, our fears, our heartaches. Because of this child, we have a sense of purpose, hope, direction and meaning to all of life's complexities. May the "language of Christmas" be yours too in the coming days.

 Notes

Winter Solstice Sunshine: Sunshine rolls across the valley at dawn, after light falls of snow overnight near Millstreet, marking the Winter Solstice.

DECEMBER 21ST

'The people that walked in darkness have seen a great light. On those who lived in a land as dark as death, a light has dawned.' –Isaiah 9:1

Today is the Winter Solstice and it's a hugely significant day. It's a day that has fascinated people for thousands of years. Before science gave us proper explanations on the way our planet tilts and changes its axis with the seasons, people feared the dark days of winter and that the world was going to end. But people began to understand that today marked a turning point. Darkness would loose its firm grip to give way to increasing light. Today also has huge spiritual significance. Every single one of us has our dark corners. On our own such darkness could overwhelm us. We need support, love, companionship, friendship, hope and light to guide us on our daily journey. At Christmas we mark the birth of Jesus who was the greatest light. Christmas can be summed up in many ways but the invitation is to invite Jesus into our own struggles and darkness. Today reminds us that in the depths of darkness there is great hope. Christmas is a celebration of this hope. Without it we have absolutely nothing.

 Notes

I love you both: Kiely Gretta Lehane with her parents Aideen and Seán at a Christmas function in Coláiste Choilm, Ballincollig

DECEMBER 22ND

A dad passed his daughter's room one night and overheard her repeating the alphabet in an oddly reverent way. 'What on earth are you up to?' he asked. 'I'm saying my prayers,' explained the little girl. 'But I can't think of exactly the right words tonight, so I'm just saying all the letters. God will put them together for me, because God knows what I'm thinking.'

We often are in a similar position. On occasions we're simply stuck for words and not sure how to express our prayers in the way we want. We're often reduced to simply holding the letters. Some don't even get that far and give up thinking it's a futile task. But holding the letters is always a good place to be. As we approach Christmas we can hold all those letters. They can include our inner-most thoughts and whatever is going on for us at the moment. They can include our loved ones, our closest friends and those who are special in our lives. They can include those who have hurt us and let us down. They can include our hopes and dreams. The letters are many. Sometimes the words come easy but if we struggle with them, let God put them together for you.

 Notes

Christmas Twins: Orla O'Shea puts together a lovely Christmas wreath at Coláiste Choilm, Ballincollig

DECEMBER 23RD

Perfection is the ability to incorporate imperfection. There's no other way to live. You either incorporate imperfection or you fall into denial. That's how the Spirit moves in or out of our lives.'
–Richard Rohr

In a Navajo rug there is always an imperfection woven into the rug. The pattern is perfect and then there's one part of it that clearly looks like a mistake. But this is part of the plan-there is no such thing as perfection. It's a mindset that Jesus would have been much closer to and one that he often worked out of. We have built everything up around perfection, especially looks, fashion and accessories. Christmas has been set up around perfection. The mindset is if you have a perfect Christmas then you'll be perfectly happy. This is false and so wide of the mark. It just can't happen. When we embrace all the imperfections in our lives and get on with the task of doing our best, then life and Christmas can take on much more meaning.

 Notes

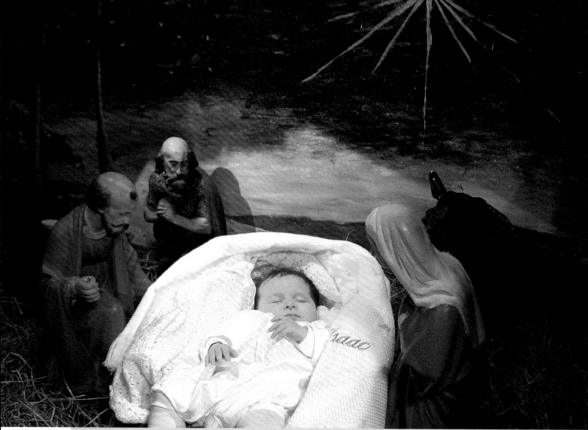

What It's All About: Isaac Jonathan O'Sullivan takes time out in the crib at the Church Of The Sacred Heart, Glounthaune

DECEMBER 24TH

'What can I give him, poor as I am? If I were a shepherd I would bring a lamb, If I were a wise man I would do my part. Yet what can I give him - give him my heart.' ~ from In the Bleak Mid Winter

What is your favourite Christmas carol? In a poll carried out recently by the BBC some of the world's leading choir masters and choral experts chose 'In the Bleak Mid Winter'. It came well ahead of well known carols such as 'Silent Night' and 'O Come All Ye Faithful'. It was written by Christiana Rosetti in 1872. As a Christmas carol it is rich in depth and meaning. The simple beauty of its content is also challenging. From the depth of wintery, cold and darkness, the invitation is to move into warmth and welcome. The carol takes us into the heart of the crib but also to the heart of whatever is going on in our lives. There God is to be found. At the heart of the bleak mid winter and on this Christmas Eve there is great hope.

 Notes

A Child Is Born: The Christmas Crib in Killarney Cathedral reminding us how special today is

DECEMBER 25TH

'An individual is harder than iron, stronger than stone and more fragile than a rose.' –Turkish Proverb

Every person is a complex mixture of strengths and weaknesses, toughness and gentleness, good points and not so good. We are delicate and fragile. Yet we are also capable of showing remarkable resilience. Everyone's personal story, beliefs and viewpoints are so varied and different. As life is complex, so are we. At the heart of the message of Christmas, God is present in the middle of all our complexities. God isn't present on the outskirts but right in the middle of whatever is going on for us. It may not be pretty, it may not be exciting, it may even be a huge struggle but that's where God wants to be. God isn't the cause of complexities but is most definitely the cause of a sense of purpose, hope, and a guiding force through these complexities. This isn't just for today Christmas Day but every single day that is God's gift to us.

 Notes

Burning Off The Christmas Dinner!: A walker makes the most of available light on the pier at Salthill, Co.Galway

DECEMBER 26TH

'There will always be a lot of 'a la carte' Christianity as long as human beings are human.' ~Liam Hickey

The famous parable of the sower reminds us that the seed was thrown everywhere and anywhere. It was thrown in hope that it might take root and then grow. Some of it did great, some did ok and some of the seed failed miserably. The seed stands for God's love and how well it's received depends entirely on the openness of people. We might think that God wants us all to be 100% open and ready. But this is not God's only way of doing things. We live in a world today where choices are vast and limitless. There is so much to choose from in terms of groceries, clothes, books, music and so on. It should come as no surprise that people will also choose when it comes to faith matters. God's generosity in throwing the seed will never stop. My openness is entirely up to me but to be open makes for great beginnings.

 Notes

Out On The Farm: It may be Christmas holidays but Ger and Daniel McSweeney make sure all the animals are fed

DECEMBER 27TH

'Trust in the Lord forever, for in the Lord God you have an everlasting rock.' ~Isaiah 26:4

Trust is something that is hugely important to us. It is not automatic. Earning trust takes time and losing trust can happen quickly. As a child we placed total trust in our parents and whoever was looking after us. Then as we journeyed through life we experienced setbacks and broken promises. Different things and events eroded our trust in others. The level of trust in society at large is also very low. For anyone who has been let down it can be hard to build the levels of trust up again. We are reminded throughout our scripture readings that God is completely trustworthy. But why do we also find it hard to trust God? Perhaps we haven't given God enough time in our lives? Perhaps God is there for us like a fire brigade, only when there is an emergency. We are encouraged to begin to put our trust in God. God will always be on our side. To believe in that is a great start.

 Notes

Taking Things Nice And Easy: These ducks remind us how important taking some time out is at this time of year!

DECEMBER 28TH

'God does not die when we cease to believe in a personal deity. We die on the day when our lives cease to be illuminated by the steady radiance, renewed daily, of a wonder, the source of which is beyond all reason.' ~Dag Hammarskjöld

Life can best be described as challenging, on occasions cruel, and rarely easy. From our own experience we know it is often unpredictable, exciting and also at times overwhelming. It would take a person of remarkable strength and zeal to journey through life on their own. We need support, love and encouragement on our journey. It's a need that must be met every day and not on the odd occasion here and there. Some of us are lucky to have this need met, others not so. The one common link we all have is our need of God. God isn't the magician who will solve our problems or make life easier. Having God on our side gives us deeper roots in life. These deeper roots give us that positive edge in everything we do each day.

 Notes

Winter Wonderland: Overnight snow transforms the landscape

DECEMBER 29TH

'A gift should be enjoyed or it can be put away and forgotten. It can challenge us, surprise us, fulfil a need or change our lives. A good gift brings joy with it. I have realised that my family and friends are not a haphazard quirk of fate, but gifts from a loving God.' ~Sue Whitehead

How often we take for granted those around us, particularly those who are generous with their time, loving and kind. Just like turning on a tap we expect the water to flow because this is what happens every time we use it. But what if the water didn't flow? What if those who are special to us simply dried up in all they give us? We would soon be lost, lonely and dispirited. There is a lovely saying that says: 'A good friend is hard to find and when you find one good and true, don't change the old one for the new.' Today I thank God for my family and friends. I thank God for their friendship and support. May I never take them for granted.

 Notes

Our Crib: Every church has its own unique crib picking up on the same story but each with its own layout, interpretation, colour and decoration like this crib in the Church Of The Annunciation, Blackpool

DECEMBER 30TH

To keep a lamp burning we have to keep putting oil in it.'~Mother Teresa

The same goes for many things in life. Whatever is special or sacred always needs nourishment and nurturing. Like the oil giving energy and life to the flame, we too need to watch what gives us life and energy. It is not an unlimited supply. If we look back on the year just gone the chances are that negative news has dominated the headlines. Negative news does drain us physically, emotionally and spiritually. It can't be avoided and it has to be faced. But it can't become our only focus each day. We've got to fight our corner and watch our space. We've got to make sure that we do things and mix with people who give us life and energy. Spiritually we can do it by connecting with God in some way. Like the wax in a candle or oil in a lamp, we believe that God is our source of inspiration, hope and energy. No one can take this source away from us. We can tap into it as little or as often

Notes

Time to reflect: A colourful robin takes time out to reflect on the year just gone

DECEMBER 31ST

'You'll learn more about a road by travelling it than by consulting all the maps in the world.'
~Author Unknown

Maps have been around for thousands of years. Today maps have been replaced more by satellite navigation systems. We're told they're more reliable and accurate in getting us to our destination. But modern technology and different maps can never tell us the feel of a road and its character. The only way to find out is by travelling along it. The same goes in life. All our journeys are uniquely different. All roads in life have their many twists and turns. Some uphill, some down, but all going in the one direction. Today is a day for looking back on our year just gone but also looking forward in hope and anticipation. With God as our map and compass, we pray for guidance and direction as we say goodbye to the year just gone and welcome in the New Year tomorrow.

 Notes